William Barnes

William Barnes

A Life of the Dorset Poet

Alan Chedzoy

THE DOVECOTE PRESS

First published in 1985 by The Dovecote Press
Stanbridge, Wimborne, Dorset

ISBN 0 946159 32 7

© Alan Chedzoy 1985

Designed by Humphrey Stone
Typesetting by Characters, Chard, Somerset
Printed and bound by Biddles Ltd,
Guildford and King's Lynn

For Brenda, Gillian, Michael
and Bobby

Contents

Acknowledgements

I should like to thank: Tom and David Fox, of the Blackmore Vale, for their unrivalled knowledge of the scenes of Barnes's childhood; Eric Hembrow for his advice on Sedgemoor dialect; Major-General E.A.W. Williams, of Herringston, Dorset, for permission to reproduce a drawing from a sketchbook by Barnes in his possession (No 2); Dr Charlotte Lindgren, of Emerson College, Boston, Massachusetts, for helping me with her expert knowledge of portraits of the Barnes family; my colleague, Dr Jim Davies, of the Dorset Institute of Higher Education, for teaching me to interpret old maps of Dorchester; two other colleagues, Furse Swann, for a suggestion concerning Gerard Manley Hopkins, and Glynn Stokes for help with Latin translations; Chris Wrigley for his kindness in reading the manuscript; Roger Peers, Curator of the Dorset County Museum, and his assistant, Paul Ensom, for much help and advice on the Barnes collection in their keeping, and for permission to reproduce copyright illustrations held by the Museum; Hugh Jacques, Dorset County Archivist, for his advice on the notebook of John Richards of Warmwell; Douglas Ashdown and Fred Langford of the William Barnes Society, for their friendly interest in all discussions concerning William Barnes; Trevor Hearl, the most assiduous of Barnes scholars, for his stimulating company and generosity in sharing ideas. All the illustrations, with the exception of numbers 2, 4, 9, 10, 11, 12 and 13, are the copyright of the Dorset Natural History and Archaeological Society, Dorset County Museum. Numbers 9 and 10 are reproduced by kind permission of the National Portrait Gallery. Lastly, I should like to thank my publisher, David Burnett of the Dovecote Press, whose meticulous reading of my typescript has been of considerable help.

AC

Introduction

In October 1886 Thomas Hardy wrote the obituary of a celebrated Dorchester figure whom he had known since he himself was a boy. In the pages of the *Athenaeum* he recollected a bearded clergyman, of great age, 'quaintly attired in caped cloak, knee-breeches and buckled shoes, with a leather satchel slung over his shoulders, and a stout staff in his hand.'[1] This anachronistic apparition was the Reverend William Barnes, the Dorset poet, who walked out regularly from Winterborne Came on market days, and who would stand a moment at the junction of Cornmarket and High West Street to set his fob watch to the 'London time' of the town clock. Dorchester today boasts two statues of literary men. Hardy sits on a plinth at Top o' Town, gazing out over the meadows to the distant ancient earthwork of Poundbury. But it is Barnes who holds the centre stage. His statue stands outside St Peter's Church, only a few steps from where he set his watch. It is as if he had decided one market day not to go home, but had instead stepped up onto his plinth, so that the life of his county might continue to swirl about him.

Barnes is chiefly remembered for his three volumes of poetry in the Dorset dialect, published in 1844, 1859 and 1862. As well as fine poetry, these books comprise a great storehouse of information on English rural life as it had existed from the time of Shakespeare until the coming of enclosures and industrialisation. Because he wrote in dialect, Barnes, far more than Crabbe or Clare, may be claimed as the authentic village voice of English poetry. His idiom is the vigorous tongue of Dorset working people, and his themes their work, play and home life. Yet he was no untutored yokel but one of the most learned of English poets, who drew upon his knowledge of Saxon, Welsh and Persian verse forms in order to shape his stanzas.

Barnes was never a best-seller, but he was probably the only poet in nineteenth century England who could regularly fill a hall with his own neighbours anxious to hear him read his work. So popular was his verse with the labouring population of Wessex that, during his later life, he received scores of invitations from working men's institutes to read to them, and the parish halls and schoolrooms were invariably crowded for these occasions. Poor rural workers would walk miles into a town to hear him and one even wrote to him to plead for a cheaper edition of his poems, so that the working folk might read him.

He also commanded a more prestigious readership. The poet laureate, Lord Alfred Tennyson, visited him at Came Rectory, and so much admired Barnes's dialect writing that he was moved to write the 'Northern Farmer' poems in his own Lincolnshire dialect. Barnes's other contemporary admirers included William Allingham, Coventry Patmore, Edmund Gosse and Francis Turner Palgrave, all of whom left memorials of this man whom the diarist, Francis Kilvert, described as 'the great idyllic Poet of England'. In our own century, Barnes's work has been admired by writers as diverse as Llewelyn Powys, E.M. Forster and Philip Larkin. Most important of all is his influence on Gerard Manley Hopkins and Thomas Hardy. Hopkins was an early admirer of Barnes and described him to Bridges as 'straight from nature and quite fresh'. In Hardy's writing Barnes is an omnipresence. So many of Hardy's themes, turns of phrase, images and ideas, seem to have their origin in something written by Barnes long before, that it was probably not possible for the younger poet consciously to estimate his debt to the elder. Barnes, quite simply, had entered his blood stream.

If this had been all, then Barnes's life story would have been worth the telling simply as that of an original and influential Victorian poet. But there is more to the story than this. Despite the fact that his days were spent entirely in small towns, his struggle with social and economic circumstances is an heroic one, and it is significant that, nine years before Hardy wrote of Jude Fawley's attempts to better himself, he could observe of Barnes's life that 'a more notable instance of self-help has seldom been recorded'. In his early days Barnes knew both poverty and joy. As a young man, he struggled hard to overcome his humble origins. His first sight of Julia Miles determined him to marry her, and the tale of their courting and idyllic wedded life is one of the triumph of human affection. Her death was for him a matter of profound and life-long grief which was compounded by professional and financial troubles, but, in all this, he continued to display high courage and an unusual integrity. As an innovative schoolmaster he was much loved by his pupils; as a clergyman, he was so highly respected by his parishioners that Dorset tradition has subsequently categorised him as a 'Worthy'. Perhaps, as twentieth century readers, we are repelled by any manifestation of moral worthiness. If so, we would do well to remind ourselves that even a good man may be a poet.

Barnes was a self-taught linguist of such range that his book *A Philological Grammar*, published in 1854, draws upon no fewer than seventy-two languages. He would pick up a language from anyone who could teach him, but usually he taught himself from a textbook. In her book, *The Life of William Barnes: Poet and Philologist*, his daughter, Lucy Baxter, observed that, if he were given a dictionary, he would usually teach himself to read a new language in a week or two. His prodigious research in philology resulted in papers and textbooks published over a time-span of more than fifty years, but almost all this vast amount of writing is concerned to argue a single case. He had loved the dialect that he heard in the Blackmore Vale as a boy and, as a scholar, he considered the Dorset dialect to be a form of the 'pure' Saxon English, which was a superior linguistic medium to the standard English of Victorian times with its heavy dependence on Latin, French and other imported terms. He therefore made a single-handed attempt to change the course of the English language away from the Latinate language of the educated classes in favour of a 'pure' Saxon English which would be comprehensible to the humblest scholar in a village school or his father and mother in church. Such an aim provoked suspicions of crankiness among fellow philologists, but it was to this grand end that he wrote his dialect poems, his books on philology and also his glossaries of the Dorset dialect which were meant to preserve valuable elements of 'pure' English.

Even his works as an historian and folklorist were designed to support his views on language. For many years he lectured and wrote on such topics as the Ancient Britons and the Saxons, and he was also a founder member of the Dorset County Museum and the Dorset Field Club. Such antiquarian activities occupied his scholarly hours in his later life at the expense of his scientific interests although, as a young man, he had written and published a book dedicated to his first tutor in mathematics, General Shrapnel, and had also been granted a special private demonstration of the workings of the electric telegraph by its inventor, Professor Wheatstone. He had also been a student of the Hindu sacred texts and the translations and commentaries he published upon them in 1839 and 1841 in *The Gentleman's Magazine* constitute an extraordinary achievement of sympathetic imaginative scholarship from an obscure country schoolmaster in the age of Trollope.

Though his fame was greater as poet and scholar, Barnes's professional life was spent first as a schoolmaster of a small private academy, and latterly as a country clergyman. Schoolmastering for him was no mere 'background' to his life as a poet. It occupied him fully and called forth the highest in his imaginative and creative powers. He invariably wrote a textbook after working up a series of lessons or lectures, and he was one of the pioneers of the school primer. He wrote texts for his classes on mathematics, history, civics, grammar, technical drawing, practical science, geography and Anglo-Saxon, which last subject he was one of the first to introduce into schools. He was an effective, sometimes a brilliant, teacher. He instituted changes in the curriculum which went as far as he dared with paying parents to please. He was a reformist in the matter of school discipline and completely disapproved of corporal punishment. During 39 years as a schoolmaster, he was never known to strike a pupil or to speak harshly to one. He numbered many famous men among his ex-pupils and these included such men of science as Octavius Pickard Cambridge, an arachnologist of world-wide authority, and Frederick Treves, surgeon to Edward VII and also to the 'Elephant Man'. In middle life Barnes became a founder and pioneer of the movement for mechanics' institutes, that great engine of working-class education. He persisted in serving this cause for over a quarter of a century, at great hazard to his own pocket and interests.

After 1862, Barnes became the Rector of Winterborne Came

and one of that band of Victorian parsons who pursued scholarship along with parochial duties. He was never a man to neglect
his responsibilities. Until well into his eighties he regularly
walked the roads of his rural parish, sometimes covering twenty
miles a day, in order to visit each parishioner at least once a
fortnight. His sermons were cast in the homely English that his
congregation could understand and he would give attention to
rehearsing the children's choir before turning to the needs of
such august visitors as Thomas Hardy and Edmund Gosse. He
cared nothing for fashion or for weathers and, when it rained,
would cover himself with an old sack, and sling his Dorchester
purchases over his shoulder in order to save the shopman the
trouble. The country people loved him and the children would
crowd round to accept the sweets he kept to distribute among
them. Like George Herbert before him, he was a country parson
widely noted for his piety and kindness to the poor. Unlike
George Herbert, he was also noted for his humour.

Despite his mildness of manner and his genuine humility,
Barnes provoked some hostility both in Mere, where he kept his
first school, and in Dorchester. This was because, though he was
gentle and respectful to all, he remained completely untouched
by the dictates of fashion and received opinion. His manners,
his mode of dress, his manner of talking to servants as to equals,
his intellectual opinions, were taken neither from Dorchester
society nor from contemporary newspapers, but were founded
upon the reading and thought of many years. He was that most
rare of creatures, a man who lives by ideas. Such a person
inevitably attracts the wrath of his neighbours because he
appears to be disdainful of their notions of propriety. Nothing
more fully exemplifies his intellectual independence than his
grand design to 'purify' the English of his day from its Latin
and French accretions. Many of his middle-class Dorchester
neighbours paid him, so they thought, to educate their sons out
of the vulgarities of dialect, while he was publishing books and
articles to prove the superiority of that dialect to 'standard'
English.

Barnes was a polymath in an age when such creatures had
become rare. No contemporary biographer can hope to follow
him throughout his studies. I am, myself, no judge of the value of

his pamphlet on the hanging of farm gates nor can I estimate the soundness of his observations upon the 72 languages drawn upon in the *Philological Grammar*. What I have tried to do is to re-read his notebooks and correspondence in the Dorset County Museum, along with his 900 or so poems and other published work, with the intention of re-interpreting his life for a modern readership. In particular, I have tried to use the poetry as biographical evidence. One major truth has become apparent to me while doing so. Almost everything Barnes wrote was in some way a celebration and defence of the way of life he knew in the Vale of Blackmore when he was a child. His dialect poems called forth the great lyrical and humorous potential of Blackmore language; his huge programme of philological research was all used to bolster his claims for the 'purity' of that language; his studies in history and antiquities were attempts to prove the foundations of Blackmore society; his works on political economy were diatribes against the nineteenth century capitalism which was sweeping away the little farmers, such as his uncle and aunt in Blackmore; his teaching of the working men of Dorset was his way of trying to strengthen this dispossessed peasantry, while his studies in folklore strove to record for ever their festivals, customs and homely beliefs. His loyalty to the peasant class was the fiercest passion in his outwardly conventional life. In temperament he was sweetly childlike with a peculiar innocence of manner that endeared him even to his scholars. Even while walking up High West Street in the dress of a Victorian clergyman, Barnes had always in him much of the yeoman-farmer's son from Bagber Common.

This life of Barnes is necessarily short and omits much detail. The Dorset County Museum has a huge collection of Barnes material from which I have room to draw only the most salient pieces of information. The reader wishing to know more of Barnes will consult the specialist monographs, listed in the bibliography, which explore his work as a linguist, schoolmaster, engraver, botanist and clergyman. In concentrating upon his life as a poet, I have tried to quote widely from his verse wherever possible, and I have provided a reference to *The Poems of William Barnes*, (1962), edited by Bernard Jones, for any poem quoted.[2]

In 1986 we celebrate the centenary of Barnes's death. No life of Barnes as a poet has been in print for some years. It seemed time to provide another for the general reader in his commemorative year.

ALAN CHEDZOY
Weymouth, 1985

1

Blackmore Vale
1801-1818

On the morning of Thursday, 30th April 1874, two men walked through the little wicket gate that always stood open in front of the old Rectory at Winterborne Came, on the road from Dorchester to Broadmayne. The solid old house, with its washed walls and thatched roofs and verandahs running round it, was the home of the parson-poet, William Barnes. His visitors were also clergymen. One was Henry Moule, Vicar of Fordington near Dorchester; the other was the diarist, Francis Kilvert, a young man of thirty-four and brim full of enthusiasm for Barnes and his works. The two visitors were greeted by Barnes at the Rectory door. His manner was gentle and courteous as he walked with his guests round the garden and sat with them in the shade of the verandah. His appearance much impressed Kilvert. His dress was of the eighteenth rather than the nineteenth century; he wore a loose gown, black knee-breeches, black silk stockings and gold-buckled shoes. As he sat talking with his guests he absent-mindedly stroked his beard so that he seemed to Kilvert to be 'half-hermit, half enchanter'.[1]

The conversation inevitably turned to the Dorset dialect poems that Barnes had published over the course of many years. He had left his childhood home in the Blackmore Vale over fifty years previously and yet these poems were full of recollections of those years, of people and places he had known as a boy. Curiously, the forty years he had spent as a schoolmaster in Mere and Dorchester had figured little in the poetry. It is as if his imagination had been untouched by the Victorian years and had remained in an earlier England, unshaped by enclosures, industrialisation and the railway. For Kilvert, as for others, he seemed to be a man from an earlier age. Barnes confided to his young visitor that his poems were nothing but recollections of those earlier times. He said that when he had written them, the familiar scenes and faces had crowded into his memory, and that 'all (he) had had to do was to write them down'.[2] In describing scenes in his verse, he added, he had always had an original place in mind, but had, at times, altered the landscape to suit his purpose.

Barnes was the first to admit the limitations in theme and inspiration of his subject matter but, paradoxically, it is its very parochialism that gives his work more than local appeal. For his poems speak for all England, its towns and villages as they had existed during the preceding three centuries since the time of Shakespeare. In his obituary of Barnes, Thomas Hardy wrote that he was 'probably the most interesting link between the present and past forms of rural life that England possessed'.[3] In Barnes's dialect poetry is to be found an entire repertory of the life, language, customs and folklore of pre-industrial England. His poetry is more informative on such matters than that of Crabbe or Clare because, unlike their verse, it memorialises that life in the authentic cadences in which it was felt and expressed. Not only are his 'Hwomely Rhymes' immensely rich in detailed observation of obscure rural lives, but they also constitute a storehouse of expression shored up against time and social change.

William Barnes was born in the Blackmore (or Blackmoor) Vale in 1801 and it was there that he spent the first eighteen years of his life. The great clay vale extends south and east of Sherborne in an arc west of Shaftesbury and up beyond the Somerset border. Through its heart flows the River Stour, fed by such tributaries as the Lydden and the Caundle brook. Perhaps the best description of it is that to be found in *Tess of the D'Urbervilles*, for Hardy placed his heroine's birthplace at Marnhull, which he renamed 'Marlott':

This fertile and sheltered tract of country, in which the fields are never brown and the springs never dry, is bounded on the south by the bold chalk ridge that embraces the prominences of Hambledon Hill, Bulbarrow, Nettlecombe-Tout, Dogbury, High Stoy, and Bubb Down. The traveller from the coast, who, after plodding northward for a score of miles over calcareous downs and corn-lands, suddenly reaches the verge of one of these escarpments, is surprised and delighted to behold,

extended like a map beneath him, a country differing absolutely from
that which he has passed through. Behind him the hills are open, the sun
blazes down upon fields so large as to give an unenclosed character to the
landscape, the lanes are white, the hedges low and plashed, the atmosphere colourless. Here, in the valley the world seems to be constructed
upon a smaller and more delicate scale; the fields are mere paddocks, so
reduced that from this height their hedgerows appear a network of dark
green threads over-spreading the pale green of the grass. The atmosphere beneath is languorous, and is so tinged with azure that what
artists call the middle distance partakes also of that hue, while the
horizon beyond is of the deepest ultramarine. Arable lands are few and
limited; with but slight exceptions the prospect is a broad rich mass of
grass and trees, mantling minor hills and dales within the major. Such is
the Vale of Blackmoor.[4]

Photographs from Victorian times reveal just how much the
Vale has changed since Barnes's day. The oak, ash and elm are
now much depleted but the country is still that of rivers and
bridges, water meadows and the Stour running down to Sturminster bearing its summer pride, the yellow water lily or 'clote',
so beloved of Barnes.

The birth of William Barnes is clearly registered in the records
of the parish of Sturminster Newton Castle and the entry is dated
29 March 1801. The total population of the parish in 1801 was
1406 and its area included the town and two or three small
hamlets beyond. Sturminster Newton is an ancient market town
which served as a centre for the commerce of the Vale. Sturminster, the more northerly settlement, is looped by the Stour;
Newton with its famous mill lies along the southern bank; the
two are linked by a six-arched mediaeval bridge. The young
William Barnes was familiar with the bridge and the mill with its
pigeon cotes, with the pedestal of the market cross, and with the
White Hart Inn and the Bull Tavern, both of which are still
standing. The parish church, St Mary's, was much altered in the
restoration of the Rev T.H. Lane Fox, shortly after he left the Vale.
Hard by the Church is the school house which he attended as a
boy and Vine House where he copied deeds for Thomas Dashwood, his first employer.

In March 1801 there was a Population Return for the parish
from which we can learn a great deal about Sturminster Newton
at the time of Barnes's birth. Of the 619 males, 310 were in work

and we may assume that the greater proportion of those remaining were juveniles. Ninety-five of the men, including John Barnes, the father of the poet, declared themselves to be 'labourers in husbandry' a phrase which might include tenant farmers, skilled farm workers and mere labourers. Fifty-three others were registered as weavers and were presumably engaged in the cottage industry manufacturing 'swanskin', the strong cloth which was exported to the Newfoundland fisheries. The Population Return suggests that Sturminster was a place of vigorous and varied local industry with a largely self-sufficient economy, as befits the 'capital' of the Vale. Apart from the males engaged in husbandry and weaving, the others participated in some forty trades, among them those of the thatcher, carpenter, miller and tanner. The town supported only 21 male paupers in the almshouse. Four inhabitants, including Dashwood, described themselves simply as 'gentlemen', while only one man described himself as a beggar. Of the 260 women at work in the town, no fewer than 195 were employed at home as spinners, 35 were servants and eight declared themselves to be 'mantua-makers'.[5] The town boasted no fewer than twelve schoolmistresses but only one schoolmaster, the redoubtable Tommy Mullett, later to teach Barnes.

Recollection is always selective. Barnes's memories of the life in his birthplace are nearly all idyllic and they formed the basis for his adult views on the nature of a healthy community and the importance of independence to give a man self-respect. In later life he often returned as a visitor to the little market town and testified to the happiness of his growing days spent there. Despite the early death of his mother, his experience of the town remained golden in his memory in after years.

How contrasting are the recollections of Robert Young ('Rabin Hill', 1811-1908), the second of Sturminster's dialect poets and a friend and near contemporary of Barnes. In 1908, the last year of his life, Robert Young wrote an account of his recollections of Sturminster as far back as the feast in 1815 given to celebrate the Battle of Waterloo. He also remembered darker things, such as the punishment of a quiet man who, unable to endure any longer the nagging of a shrewish wife, left for Poole, thus making her a charge upon the parish. When he was brought back to Sturminster

he was stripped, strapped to a wheel, and flogged to the accom-
paniment of screaming, fainting women. Unlike Young, Barnes
did not seem to notice the drunkenness and brutality, the filthy
hovels on the outskirts of the town, or the dreadful poverty of
whole families forced to live upon a labourer's pay of seven
shillings (35p) a week.

The exact place and date of Barnes's birth are both matters for
dispute. All authorities are agreed that his birthplace was at
Bagber Common, about a mile and a half west of Sturminster
Newton, but the actual building is still a matter of doubt. The
registration of his birth on 29 March 1801 gives his parents as
John and Grace Barnes but the birthplace is not named, only
listed as building number seven. In her life of her father, Lucy
Baxter names his birthplace as 'Rushay', a farm not far from
Pentridge. The original building has been largely demolished
but there is still a farm-house at Rushay lying beside the long
drove onto the common. A local resident of Bagber, Mr Stanley
Duffett, still remembers that his grandfather referred to a
meadow north of Rushay as 'Barnes's Orchard' while a tree in
one of the hedgerows is known locally as 'Barnes's Oak'. Lucy
Baxter also reported that the family moved soon after William's
birth to a house called 'Golden Gate'. Nothing remains of this
house but an embankment and a ditch which might have served
to mark the limits of the property. The precise movements of the
family round about the beginnings of the nineteenth century
will probably never be established, but it seems likely that the
'Orchard' marked the site of an earlier home from which there
were two movements, the first to Rushay and then to the Golden
Gate.[6]

Bagber itself was a much bleaker place than Sturminster, just a
hamlet of a few houses belonging to farm workers, dairy-men
and graziers, the Rabbets, Bullens, Moores and Jeanes; the
Plummers, Lees, Barneses and Cluetts. Much of their food they
supplied themselves. In his book *The State of the Poor*, written in
1797, Sir Frederick Morton Eden[7] revealed that the staple fare of a
labourer's family in the south and west of England at the end of
the eighteenth century was bread supplemented with cheese,
milk, broth, potatoes and occasionally a little meat. The Barnes
family at Rushay Farm were never poor, perhaps, but their diet

can have been little better than that described by Eden. Wages
for farm workers in Dorset were notoriously low and there is no
reason to believe that the employees of George Pitt, the second
Lord Rivers, were paid better than most. What would have
supplemented the incomes and the diets of these labouring
families was the produce of the common land itself, which
offered grazing for geese and swine, patches of cultivated land
for garden produce, furze for firing and space for exercise and
festival. It was the common land that preserved some independence for such labourers in husbandry as John Barnes.

It was in this poor place, in a cottage of cob and thatch, that
William Barnes was born. All the authorities save Thomas Hardy
believe him to have been born in 1801 through Hardy says 1800.
Giles Dugdale has argued persuasively that it is most unlikely
that the registration of a child's birth should be delayed for a
year, particularly if the child were thought to be delicate, as was
the case with William Barnes.[8] As for the date in 1801, Dugdale
had direct contact with members of the family of the poet and
learned from them that his birthday was traditionally celebrated
on February 22, so this must be assumed to be the most likely
date.

The Barneses were a 'downstart' family. Lucy Baxter has
sketched out the story of the family's decline and her account
must have been the version accepted substantially by her father.
She tells of a certain William Barnes, perhaps originating from
Barnes in Surrey, who was awarded a grant of land at Gillingham
in Dorset from Henry VIII in 1540. Barnes's descendants
flourished for a time: George Barnes possessed lands at Bourton,
Shearstock and Gillingham and his son, John, became the 'head
borough' of Gillingham in 1604. Then followed two generations
of John Barneses to be succeeded by a Jerome who was probably
the wealthiest of all the Barneses and owned land in Todber and
East Stour, and even Hampshire. His son, another Jerome, held
the land of a farm named 'Mageston', and was succeeded by two
generations of Johns, the second of whom was the poet's grandfather.

It is with John Barnes, the grandfather, that the decline of the
family's fortune truly begins. He should have inherited the land
at East Stour, close to Gillingham, but it was lost about 1732

when his own father died young and left the estate in irrespon-
sible hands. Nevertheless, this John Barnes grew up to hold the
farm at Manston but again death struck at the family for both he
and his wife died young and on the same day, in a smallpox
outbreak in 1776, leaving three daughters and a son, John, the
father of the poet. Again, the estate was placed in the care of a
relative, this time an uncle of the children, but, as William
Barnes recalls, the farm was 'wasted' and the children left almost
destitute. Furthermore, John Barnes knew nothing of farm
management and was fitted to do little but help others. He was
reduced, therefore, to being the 'labourer in husbandry' that he
described himself to be, a small tenant farmer who probably
undertook work for Lord Rivers or other more affluent neighbours. William Barnes retold the tale of the loss of his family's
property in the poem *Gwain to Brookwell:*

> At Harwood Farm we pass'd the land
> That father's father had in hand,
> An' there, in open light did spread
> The very groun's his cows did tread,
> An' there above the stwonen tun
> Avore the dazzlen mornen zun,
> Wer still the rollen smoke, the breath
> A-breath'd vrom his wold house's he'th;
> An' there did lie below the door,
> The drashol' that his vootsteps wore;
> But there his meäte an' he bwoth died,
> Wi' hand in hand, an' zide by zide;
> Between the seäme two peals a-rung,
> Two Zundays, though they wer but young,
> An' laid in sleep their worksome hands,
> At rest vrom tweil wi' house or lands.
> Then vower children laid their heads
> At night upon their little beds,
> An' never rose ageän below
> A mother's love, or father's ho:
> Dree little maïdens, small in feäce,
> An' woone small bwoy, the fourth in pleäce.
> Zoo when the heedvul father died,
> He call's his brother to his zide,
> To meäke en stand, in his own stead.
> His children's guide, when he wer dead;

But still avore zix years brought round
The woodland goo-coo's zummer sound,
He weästed all their little store,
An' hardship drove em out o' door,
To tweil till tweilsome life should end,
'Ithout a single e'thly friend.[9]

Barnes never forgot the loss of the family property and, in later years, managed to retrieve a small part of it. It is interesting that the more noteworthy of the dialect words employed in this poem ('tun'=chimney, 'he'th'=hearth, 'drashol'=threshold) are all closely employed in the identification of the hearth with the home. When Barnes's emotions are fully engaged by recollection or sentiment they move naturally towards expression in dialect.

William Barnes was fortunate in that his parents had complementary personalities and influenced him in contrasting ways. Since he had lost his inheritance of the Manor Farm at Manston, John Barnes had only the tenancy of the 'farmling' at Bagber. He was, by all accounts, a sensible and reliable man, noted for his honesty and good-heartedness. He was born in 1763 and died in 1846 at the age of eighty-three.

Grace Barnes had been born Grace Scott at Fifehead Neville and Barnes confided to Lucy Baxter that his mother had been a woman of 'refined taste with a love of art and poetry'. She had apparently encouraged her young son's premature interest in drawing when he chalked figures on the flagstone floor. Years after he remember her as a slim young woman leading him by the hand to view figures cast in molten lead which decorated the parapet of a bridge. He knew that she had grieved over his delicacy of physique, and his long tapering fingers, which she regarded as too slender to support the rough work of a farm. She died when he was about five years old but he remembered her always and there were faded samplers she had worked on the wall of the bedroom in which he died in 1886. He long searched for some satin shoes of hers by which he hoped to commemorate her. Though he failed to find them, he wrote a poem, *Grammer's Shoes*[10], which served the same purpose. His father received a tribute in the poem *A Good Father* in which he asserts the possibilities of friendship between fathers and sons.[11]

John and Grace Barnes had six children in all, of which William
was the fifth. His brothers John, Charles and James lived into
adult life but there is no record of a intimacy with any of them
either in his childhood or later. After the death of their mother he
was probably often in the charge of his sister, Anne, who later
died in childbirth. The youngest of the family, Henry, was said
by William to have died from a chill on drinking too much cold
water in a high heat, an incident which is partly re-enacted in the
tragic poem *The Child and the Mowers*.[12]

As a child William Barnes was physically delicate and tem-
peramentally repulsed by the cunning and callousness that were
part of everyday village life. His poem, *False-Friends Like*, successfully combines self-mockery and the analysis of that diffi-
dence with which he responded to all unkindness:

> When I wer still a bwoy, an' mother's pride,
> A bigger bwoy spoke up to me so kind-like,
> 'If you do like, I'll treat ye wi' a ride
> In theäse wheel-barrow here. Zoo I wer blind-like
> To what he had a-worken in his mind-like,
> An' mounted vor a passenger inside;
> An' comen to a puddle, perty wide,
> He tipp'd me in, a-grinnen back behind-like.
> Zoo when a man do come to me so thick-like,
> An' sheäke my hand, where woonce he pass'd me by,
> An' tell me he would do me this or that,
> I can't help thinken o' the big bwoy's trick-like.
> An' then, vor all I can but wag my hat
> An' thank en, I do veel a little shy.[13]

The shyness confessed by this poem was that same emotion
which induced him to disregard the cruelties of the life around
him. As an old man he would not allow one of his daughters to
read out of the newspaper accounts of human wickedness for he
just could not bear to contemplate them, so sensitive was his
nature. He preferred as a child to sketch the beauties of the Vale
and to cherish memories of his mother whom, as might be
expected, he came to idealise. The attitude to women engendered
by his brief childhood in her care came later to inform the loving
fidelity he was to offer Julia Miles, his future wife, both throughout her life and even beyond.

It was the Rabbetts who saved him from a solitary childhood. His father's sister, 'Aunt Ann', had married Charles Rabbetts in 1780 and they lived at Pentridge Farm, hard by the River Stour, with their six boys, two girls and two servants. It was a large, merry family and served as a second home to William who must have been placed in the charge of Aunt Ann on many an occasion. A seventh Rabbett boy, Charlie, was born in the same year as William, and their births were registered on the same page. Charlie was his special friend and together the boys wandered the meadows down to the mill at Hinton St Mary and lived the life of adventurous boyhood with a freedom unknown to most modern children. William had two aunts at Pentridge, for not only was there the gentle Aunt Ann but also his unmarried Aunt Jane, or Jenny, another of his father's sisters, who was one of the household 'servants' domiciled at Pentridge. Aunt Jenny was as good-hearted as her sister but she was also renowned for her sharp tongue and sharper temper which her nephew long after commemorated in the poem *Aunt's Tantrums*[14]. Uncle Charles was remembered by Barnes as a warm-hearted, merry and generous man.

Charles and Ann Rabbetts were the originals of the 'Uncle and Aunt' of a number of poems. They served Barnes as the ideal types of cheerful, independent tenant farmers, homely in their manners, generous to their workpeople and innocent in their pride of possession:

UNCLE AN' AUNT

How happy uncle us'd to be
O' zummer time, when aunt an' he
O'Zunday evenens, eärm in eärm,
Did walk about their tiny farm,
While birds did zing an' gnats did zwarm,
Drough grass a'most above their knees,
An' roun' by hedges an' by trees
　Wi' leafy boughs a-swaÿen.

His hat wer broad, his cwoat wer brown,
Wi' two long flaps a-hangen down;
An' vrom his knee went down a blue
Knit stocken to his buckled shoe;
An' aunt did pull her gown-taïl drough
Her pocket-hole, to keep en neat,
As she mid walk, or teäke a seat
　By leafy boughs a-swaÿen.[15]

The poems devoted to Uncle and Aunt are deeply affectionate
and tinged with a little sadness. Barnes loved to dwell upon the
spontaneous joy of their life together. Years later, in *Pentridge by
the River*, he mused upon the transience of the life that was led
there. The farmhouse had been demolished and only the name
remained, yet that name for him brought back the sweetest of
memories. [16] A further portrait of Uncle and Aunt appears in
Week's End in Zummer in the Wold Vo'k's Time but here the stress is
very much upon the usefulness of the couple, both as employers
and neighbours. Unlike the more affluent farmers of later times,
Uncle and Aunt sat and ate with their workpeople and shared
their joys and griefs:

> His aunt an' uncle, — ah! the kind
> Wold souls be often in my mind:
> A better couple never stood
> In shoes, an' vew be vound so good.
> *She* cheer'd the work-vo'k in their tweils
> Wi' timely bits an' draps, an' smiles;
> An' *he* païd all o'm at week's end,
> Their money down to goo an' spend.
> In zummer, when week's end come roun',
> The hay-meäkers did come vrom groun',
> An' all zit down, wi' weary bwones,
> Within the yard a-peäved wi' stwones,
> Along avore the peäles, between
> The yard a-steän'd an' open green.
> There women zot wi' beäre-neck'd chaps,
> An' maidens wi' their sleeves an' flaps
> To screen vrom het their eärms an' polls,
> An' men wi' beards so black as coals:
> Girt stocky Jim, an' lanky John,
> An' poor wold Betty dead an' gone;
> An' cleän-grown Tom so spry an' strong,
> An' Liz the best to pitch a zong,
> That now ha' nearly half a score
> O' children zwarmen at her door;
> An' whindlen Ann, that cried wi' fear
> To hear the thunder when 'twer near, —
> A zickly maïd, so peäle's the moon,
> That voun' her zun goo down at noon;
> An' blushen Jeäne so shy an' meek,

That seldom let us hear her speak,
That wer a-coorted an' undone
By Farmer Woodley's woldest son;
An' after she'd a-been vorzook,
Wer voun' a-drown'd in Longmeäd brook.[17]

Barnes's poetry contains many such observations on the people of the Vale but he gives even greater attention to the beauties of the countryside along the banks of the Stour, which he absorbed almost without knowing it, as he shouted and ran with Charlie Rabbetts, climbed trees, stole eggs and gathered the clustering hazels in autumn. As he wandered the river bank his eye was caught by the spreading beds of the 'clote' or yellow water lily, or the clustered white of the water crowfoot; he learned to love the bending bulrush and the sedge, the 'Goocoo flower' or Ladies smock and the Yellow flag iris.

The touchstone whereby to test such influences in the growth of a poet's mind is, of course, in Wordsworth's *Prelude*. Barnes, like Wordsworth, 'held unconscious intercourse with Beauty' and drank in 'pure organic pleasure' from the landscape. For him also 'the earth and common face of nature' spake 'rememberable things'.[18] There, however, the resemblance ended. Barnes, unlike Wordsworth, was born of people who worked the fields. The 'things' nature spoke to him were not transcendental or mystical experiences, but an acquaintance with familiar scenes, actual trees which he came to know almost as individuals, the cadences and tones of voice employed by particular people. Years later he recollected these things in his poetry and, such was his feeling for them, he was able to endow his common experiences with imaginative value.

In his 'Fore-Say' to Udal's *Dorsetshire Folk-Lore*, first published in 1922, long after Barnes's death, the Dorset poet recollected that the toys and implements of his boyhood were not bought, but fashioned at home:

We, as boys, braided fishing lines of white horsehair, and made floats for them and hung them on a peeled withy wand, and made small rush baskets for our fish. Of a very roomy one we did not feel the want; and almost anybody could make a good whistle-pipe by drawing off the rind of a clean length of sappy ashen rod, and setting in a piece of wood as

a heading of the usual knit above the breath-hole. Our handskill did not
reach so far as to cut a very good top without a lathe, but we knew that an
eelskin would make a very good topwhip. To this level of folk-lore
belonged the knowledge of the rules of children's games.[19]

His earliest recollections included an incident in which he
launched a 'fleet' on the Stour, the shipping comprising himself
in a tub towing an arch-backed cat in a wooden bowl, spitting
with terror.

According to Lucy Baxter, his mother's concern at his frailty
had found reassurance in the words of the 'wise women' of the
village, one of whom had declared that William had been born
with a silver spoon in his mouth and another that the mother was
not to worry for he would get his living by 'learning books and
such like'. Another of his daughters, Laura, was told a rather
different story in that the person who predicted a future of books
and learning was Jemmy Jenkins, a local magician, whose collection of over two hundred books on magic and astrology first
roused Barnes's prodigious passion for reading. Apparently
John Barnes had forbidden his boy to visit Jenkins but William
persisted in calling upon him and eventually had learned enough
of his secrets to earn the nickname of 'The Little Astrologer'. The
existence of wise men and women in the countryside was
common in those days. Thomas Hardy may have found inspiration in Barnes's recollections in creating Mr Fall in *The Mayor of
Casterbridge* and Conjuror Trendle in *The Withered Arm*. One of
Barnes's most memorable poems, *A Witch*, presents a somewhat
humorous picture of such an old woman and the havoc she can
create with her 'evil wish'.[29]

Early in life William Barnes exhibited artistic talents and later
on he revealed musical gifts as well. We know of the chalk
drawings he made upon the flagstones which his mother praised
when he was little. As a boy he drew pencil portraits of friends
and neighbours and sold these for a penny, twopence or threepence. The portraits must have had some accuracy for him to
command those prices in an impoverished market. His greatest
artistic achievement in youth was the signboard he painted for
the Black Horse Inn which was exhibited at Shrodon Fair. He
also made a sundial at the age of eleven and this was later much
prized by Henry Lane Fox who became the vicar of St Mary's.

If his artistic efforts were a matter of pride to his family, it seems likely that his first attempts at writing poetry were discouraged. The evidence for this comes in a poem entitled *The Young Rhymer Snubbed* which is so authentic in tone that it must contain a fair proportion of personal experience. Bookish pursuits must have seemed sadly irrelevant to labouring folk struggling to make a living on the edges of a common. What is characteristic in Barnes's account is that there is no reproach for those who tried to repress his poetic instinct; indeed, his humorous and essentially practical muse seems almost to take their side in the matter. The joke is, however, a paradoxical one, because the poem in which the situation is described is so very successful:

> To meäke up rhymes my mind wer zoo a-vire
>   Twer idle work to try to keep me quiet,
> O' meäken rhymes my heart did never tire;
>   Though I should never be a gaïner by it.
> 'You meäke up rhyme!' vo'k zaid, 'why who would buy it?
>   Could you write fine enough to please a squire?
>   An' rhyme's what plaïn vo'k woudden much require;
> You'd vind your rhymes would eärn but scanty diet,
> An' if I'd any cure vor it, I'm sure I'd try it.'
>
> An' father too, in learnen noo great crammer,
>   Zaid rhymen wer a treäde but vew got fat in;
> That men wi' neämes a-ringen wi' a clamour
>   Did live in holes not fit to put a cat in,
> An' sleep on locks o' straw, or bits o' matten;
>   An' mother zaid she'd sooner hear me stammer
> Than gauk about a-gabblen rhymes an' Latin.
> I'd better crack my noddle wi' her patten,
> She used to zay, or crack en wi' a hammer,
> Than vill en up wi' rhymes, an' silly stuff o'grammar.
>
> My father didden rhymy. He knew better.
>   Bezides his business, an' to buy an' zell,
> He only learnt to write a friend a letter,
>   That always went a-hopen he wer well;
> Or in a ledger, or a bill, to tell
>   Vor what an' when a man became his debtor;
>   An' mother too, I never shall vorget her,
> Wer only just a-taught to read an' spell,
> An' mark a teäble-cloth or napkin pretty well.

An' zoo I vound my friends think all the seäme o't,
  That rhyme won't vill the pocket over tight,
But then my heart did kindle wi' the fleäme o't,
  Whenever I did zee a touchen zight,
  An' I did all but lose my wits there-right.
  'Tis likely I shall meäke a losen geäme o't,
    But still, ageän, to lighten off the bleäme o't,
  Vor all do keep me poor, it still will bring
  My heart a pleasure that do leäve noo sting.[21]

The contradictions go further than this and multiply in a number of linguistic ironies. Right at the outset Barnes was forced to meet the challenge that in both language and social position he was unfitted to be a poet. The dialect spoken in the poem by the 'vo'k' around him carries with it a syllogistic commonsense which he will need to refute if he is to become a poet. That common-sense says: 'We are all dialect speakers; it is common knowledge that the language of poetry cannot be written in the dialect to which you are confined; therefore, you will never be a poet'. Barnes's method of combating this argument is simply by producing an effective poem of considerable technical accomplishment. The line: 'My father didden rhymy. He knew better.' will usually raise a laugh from an audience because of its assured worldly-wise ignorance; but the laugh is against 'my father' because the poem manifests the delights of perceptive observation of human character and also of vigorous and pithy language while pretending to deride such qualities. It is Barnes who has the last laugh but, as always, it is an affectionate one.

Formal education for Barnes began at a dame-school, no doubt kept by one of the twelve women who, in 1801, had declared themselves to be schoolmistresses. He went on to Sturminster Newton Endowed School and walked two miles each day to get there. The building still stands in a quiet close near to St Mary's Church in the north of the town. It was at this school that he gained the interest of three men rather out of the ordinary. The master was Thomas (Tommy) Mullett, renowned as an able mathematician. It was he who supplied the young Barnes with what Giles Dugdale has called 'a grounding of education which was thorough and systematic' and which helped him to acquire 'those habits of application which made it possible for him to continue his self-education afterwards'.[22] Tom Spinney, the church organist, was Barnes's first music teacher and tutored him privately in singing and the violin. In her life of her father, Lucy Baxter asserts that the Rev T.H. Lane Fox was also important in helping Barnes at this time by teaching him Latin and lending him books. This statement must be treated with caution for Lane Fox did not become curate of St Mary's until 1824, six years after Barnes left the area. Furthermore, Lane Fox was only five or six years older than Barnes, a rather narrow age gap to support Baxter's suggestion that the one acted as paternal tutor to the other.[23]

Lane Fox was one of the Pitt Rivers family. His uncle, Lord Rivers, owned a family home in Yorkshire but lived mostly at the Manor House, Hinton St Mary, where, in 1827, he died a seventy-eight year old bachelor. As the youngest son of Rivers's third sister, Lane Fox inherited from his uncle a personal fortune of some £100,000, worth at least a million in the 1980's. In 1839 Lane Fox became vicar of St Mary's, Sturminster Newton, and personally subscribed about £40,000 to the church improvements. He was also generally acknowledged to be a most liberal and humane man who supported many good causes until his death in 1861. In particular he favoured education. He was a patron of the Endowed School and he and his friend, the lawyer, Dashwood, were founders of the local evening institute.

In later life Barnes frequently referred to Lane Fox as 'the good clergyman' and occasionally stayed with him in his visits to the Vale. It is possible that Lane Fox had tutored Barnes long before he himself became the curate of St Mary's, but it is more likely that Lucy Baxter has mistakenly placed her father's acquaintance with him at an earlier time than was the case. There is no doubt, however, that Lane Fox's philanthropy and passion for education were powerful influences upon Barnes.

At school Barnes was a great favourite. One old lady who was his schoolmate remembered that he 'excelled all others and outstripped them by far'. She remembered that both the boys and the girls were quite willing to fight for him and to protect him.[24] There can be no doubt that he surpassed his fellows in most pursuits, but it is not clear whether it was his beautiful handwriting or his skill as an artist that won him his first job. He left school at thirteen to join the solicitor, Thomas Dashwood of Vine House, as an engrossing clerk. Though illness crippled his hand in middle age, we still have enough examples of Barnes's writing in youth and early manhood to know that it was extraordinarily regular and pleasing. In his obituary in the *Athenaeum*, Thomas Hardy suggests that sometime in 1814 or 1815, Dashwood entered the school and enquired if there were a boy present with handwriting good enough to copy deeds. In the subsequent writing competition imagined by Hardy, William Barnes received the laurel and the post. This story is contradicted by local tradition, especially by the account given by the late Mark Lemon to Trevor Hearl: 'While crossing a field (Mr Dashwood) saw a boy who had been sent to clear the meadow of cow dung. Instead, he had turned his wheelbarrow on its side and was sitting on it sketching a cow. Mr Dashwood admired the drawing, became interested in the artist and took him into his office . . .'[25] Dashwood became his patron as well as his employer. With his help, and that of such men as Tommy Mullett, Sturminster Newton provided a great deal of encouragement and education for Barnes which enabled him to develop his intellectual and artistic tastes despite the relatively humble and unlettered home from which he came.

The climax to Barnes's childhood days in Blackmore came with the peace celebrations that took place in Gough's Close, Sturminster, in August 1814. His prose account of the proceedings appeared in *Hone's Year Book* for 1832:

The celebration of Peace, in August, 1814, took place when I was a boy, old enough to enjoy the merry doings at my native village, and to remember them till now. The respectable inhabitants subscribed largely to treat the poor with a public dinner of beef and pudding, and strong beer. Their festival was held in a field by the river side, where several hundreds of people, young and old, sat down at two long lines of tables. Their hearing was gratified by the lively music of a band; and their taste and smell by the savour of a wholesome old English meal, at which they held their noses for an hour over the steam of boiled beef, or thrust them at intervals into the cool deepening vacuum of the beer jug. Their sight was afterwards indulged with spectacles of village merry-making; and their feelings by the twistings and twinings, and spirit-stirring hop, skip, and jump agitations of the dance.[26]

In 1859, in his second collection of poems in the Dorset dialect, Barnes gave a poetic account of the same event in *Bishop's Caundle:*

> An' while they took, wi' merry cheer,
> Their pleäces at the meat an' beer,
> The band did blow an' beät aloud
> Their merry tuens to the crowd;
> An' slowly-zwingen flags did spread
> Their hangen colors over head.
> An' then the vo'k, wi' jaÿ an' pride,
> Stood up in stillness, zide by zide,
> Wi' downcast heads, the while their friend
> Rose up avore the teäble's end,
> An' zaid a timely greäce, an' blest
> The welcome meat to every guest.
> An' then arose a mingled naïse
> O' knives an' pleätes, an' cups an' traÿs,
> An' tongues wi' merry tongues a-drown'd
> Below a deaf'nen storm o' sound.
> An' zoo, at last, their worthy host
> Stood up to gi'e em all a twoast,
> That they did drink, wi' shouts o' glee,
> An' whirlen eärms to dree times dree.[27]

The two passages are instructive in what they reveal of the differences between his early prose style and his mature verse. Furthermore, the detailed observation in the verse provides concrete evidence of Barnes's claim to be among the most significant of our social historians in poetry.

The picture of innocent merrymaking presented in this writing symbolises Barnes's memories of life in the Vale, with neighbour sitting by neighbour all along the board set amid the fields in a golden summer of thanksgiving and festival. After the Napoleonic wars English agriculture was subjected to fierce competition when once again foreign wheat could find access to English ports. The result was an agricultural depression which forced many a small man out of his farm. Uncle and Aunt were to lose Pentridge and Aunt Ann was to die of the grief of it. Bagber Common was largely enclosed so that proud independent farmers were forced to become day-labourers, hired men, or else to find no work at all.

Such things were in the future, however, when the Barneses, the Rabbetts and their neighbours met together to hang Boney in Gough's Close. From where he sat at the trestle table, William Barnes could see almost the whole of his world, his family and friends, the fields and church tower and the horizon of blue hills. South of those hills was Dorchester, the county town, and the great world where a man might read Latin and Greek and do more interesting things than mind cows or copy deeds. Years later, perhaps recalling Barnes, Thomas Hardy depicted Jude Fawley as a boy who had struggled to acquire some sort of education in his small circle of working people. Jude too had snatched some knowledge of classical languages and seized on every bit of intelligence from a stranger. He longed to leave his village for Christminster, a place where 'without fear of farmers, or hindrance, or ridicule, he could watch and wait, and set himself to some mighty undertaking like the men of old.' As he walks his mind works upon the idea of Christminster shimmering in the distance:

> 'It is a city of light,' he said to himself.
> 'The tree of knowledge grows there,' he added a few steps further on.
> 'It is a place that teachers of men spring from and go to.'
> 'It is what you might call a castle, manned by scholarship and religion.'
> After this figure he was silent a long while, till he added:
> 'It would just suit me.'[28]

When Thomas Dashwood died in 1817, Barnes left Blackmore to go to Dorchester. He was never to live in the Vale again.

2

The Poet Laureate of Dorchester
1818-1823

In 1784 the old glass-covered cupola of the market-house on Cornhill in Dorchester became dangerous and the whole structure was pulled down and replaced by an obelisk right up against the town pump. It became the centre of William Barnes's world when he first arrived from Sturminster and, indeed, for the rest of his life. Even when he lived outside the county for a few years, at Mere, it was Dorchester that called to him, while he imagined the bustling life round the pump where South Street met High West and East Streets at right angles. The town seemed a large place to him compared with Sturminster Newton. It consisted of not one but three parishes and the churches of Holy Trinity, St Peter's and All Saints huddled closely together down the hill traversed by the continuous thoroughfare of High West and East Streets. The combined parishes had a population of 2,693 in 1821, almost twice as great as that of Sturminster even without counting that of St George's, Fordington, which at that date lay outside the walls of Dorchester itself.

When, in Hardy's novel, *The Mayor of Casterbridge*, Elizabeth-Jane and her mother first spy the town after their prolonged travels, it seems an old-fashioned place to them. To Barnes, on the other hand, it seemed very go-ahead, with its regular coach services to London and Weymouth, its theatre and its famous 'Walks' – the avenues of chestnut and lime planted on the walls of the ancient town. On market day William could stroll down from the lodgings he shared with William Carey in High West Street, squeeze past the stalls outside St Peter's Church and turn left into North Square so that he might gaze out over the valley of the Frome. If the sights of the shambles distressed him on the street, he might to return to the main street to loiter outside the windows of Criswick's book-shop, or to take his walk up South

Street and as far out on the Weymouth Road as the Roman amphitheatre at Maumbury Ring. It was here, the locals told him with a certain satisfied grimness, that Mary Channing had been burnt in 1705, in front of 7000 people, for having poisoned her husband.[1]

Yet, as a country boy, Barnes felt at home in Dorchester from his first days, for it was a country town and even its busiest streets were nowhere far from the fields. St Peter's Church tower was but a stone's throw from the water meadows of the Frome to the north, where the grass was annually flooded so that the cattle might be grazed till Christmas. The King's Arms and the Antelope Hotels were both handy to the markets so that farmers might refresh themselves without inconvenience after a day's business. Carrier's vans ran a regular service to surrounding villages such as Puddletown, Charminster and Radipole. The horses were tethered with their forelegs on the pavements so that, as Hardy remarked, 'they nipped little boys by the shoulder who were passing to school'.[2] Pigs were penned in the main streets and flocks of Dorset Horns driven up to Top'oTown towards Bridport. At haymaking, the great wains lumbered past St Peter's with their towering burdens. Thomas Hardy noted that the very shops were full of bill-hooks, butter-firkins, wheelbarrows and horse embrocation. In autumn, Henchard's honest little borough displayed many an open front door, each of which revealed a tunnel of darkness as frame to the blazing colours from back gardens stocked with fuchsias, geraniums and dahlias.[3]

There was much in Dorchester to give delight to a studious young man thirsting for learning and culture. Dorchester was the county town, and many landowners kept town houses there, so that the place had become a centre for concerts and bookshops, solicitors and schools. The town had grown up upon the ruins of the old Roman settlement of Durnovaria and had much to appeal to the historical imagination. Close to its centre stood the old Crown Court which, some ten years after Barnes was to leave the town, became the focus of national interest when it staged the trial of six labouring men from the obscure village of Tolpuddle. Dorchester had been a centre of dissent and rebellion against the King in the civil war and had been strong for Monmouth in the Rebellion of 1685. When the notorious Judge Jeffreys had come to preside over the court trying Monmouth's supporters, he had been seen to laugh aloud at a sermon in which an earnest clergyman had extolled the sweetness of Christian mercy; he had then gone on to condemn twenty-nine men and women to death in a day. What a place Dorchester was to kindle visions of the past! Even when he first walked its streets in 1818 as a newcomer to the town, the young lawyer's clerk must have thought that what was really needed in Dorchester was a museum!

For five years between 1818 and 1823, William Barnes lived in Dorchester working as a clerk for the lawyer, Mr Coombs. His employer was kind and encouraged his studies just as Dashwood had done at Sturminster. The Rector of St Peter's Church, Henry John Richman, also helped the young man by allowing him access to his private library and by providing tuition in the classics. Richman had been the headmaster of the local grammar school and had been a boy at Winchester College where he had been subjected to much bullying and hard-usage. The result had been to add a degree of timidity to his natural sweetness of nature. Richman never employed corporal punishment as a schoolmaster himself. These solicitors and clergymen, Dashwood and Coombs, Lane Fox and Richman, set standards of gentility and piety which the young Barnes was eager to achieve. The boy whom Dashwood found in a field having been sent to clear cow pats was of little difference in social status from John Clare, the ploughman poet from Northamptonshire. Yet, even after his London success as a poet, Clare remained a field worker. Barnes, on the other hand, was from the first, deeply concerned to establish himself as a professional man; to attain an income and status which would satisfy his keen awareness of the notion of social respectability. This early Victorianism in his sensibility enabled him, through a life of intense self-help and study, to attain a high level of intellectual awareness. Nevertheless, it also set limits to his development as a poet from which he was able to free himself only by the adoption of dialect as his chosen medium of expression.

Barnes and his fellow lodger, William Gilbert Carey, shared a life of studious but light-hearted industry. They took bed and board above Mr Hazard's pastry-cook shop in High West Street for seven guineas a quarter. Carey, who was to become the

Clerk to the County Court at Calne, Wiltshire, was just the kind of pleasant earnest young man suited to be Barnes's companion. He too was imbued with the notion of getting on through hard study and industry. An even more important friend to William was Edward Fuller who shared his interests in music and French conversation. The two of them formed a quartet with the Zill-woods, brother and sister, and Fuller played the flute while Barnes began to exercise a new-found talent on the violin. He had started to study Italian and even to translate Petrarch and Metastasio. Richman inspired in Barnes an interest in archaeo-logy, and an awareness of the richness of the antiquity of the town. The move to Dorchester had proved a beneficial one. At the age of eighteen he found himself in a society of earnest, kindly people, devoted to a range of interests which he found new and exciting. Even at this age, however, he was beginning to show signs of that prodigious appetite for scholarship which were to mark him off from his contemporaries for the rest of his life.

Yet his creative interests in poetry and art were initially stimu-lated not by scholarship but by love. The tale shall be told in the words of his daughter, Lucy:

'One day, not many months after young Barnes arrived in Dorchester, he was walking up the High Street, when the stage-coach drew up with a great dash and clatter of the hoofs of steaming horses. William Barnes paused to see the passengers alight. From the seat behind the driver a family party descended; first a portly, matronly lady, and then the lithe figures of two young girls, one of whom, a slight, elegant child of about sixteen, sprang easily down with a bright smile. She had blue eyes and wavy brown hair, and wore a sky-blue 'spencer', (which was the name our grandmothers gave to a jacket,) and at sight of her the incipient poet felt his heart suddenly awaken to poesy. He has often told his children that the unbidden thought came into his mind 'that shall be my wife'.[4]

The younger of the two girls was called Julia Miles. Her father was James Camford Miles, an excise officer who, at that time, was removing from Cambridge to Dorchester. Barnes had no difficulty in making Julia's acquaintance, for he saw her many times in the streets and eventually invited her to a concert and later to walks in the countryside. Unfortunately for him, her

parents were not in favour of the friendship. James Miles was the
father of ten children, eight of them boys. He certainly could not
afford a dowry for his daughter and what would be her future
with an impecunious clerk of no family and no prospects? He
advised his daughter against the match and was not 'at home' to
Barnes when he called. Eventually, the two men took to cutting
each other in the street.

James Miles must have felt that he could not afford to allow
Julia the indulgence of this relationship. In the County Museum
in Dorchester there is a letter dated 13 October 1906 in which
Barnes' daughter, Laura, wrote to tell her brother, William Miles
Barnes, what she knew of their mother's family. She was able to
offer only vague recollections that 'Mother's brothers were
brought up in a careless way.' The boys were endowed with
splendid first names: Frederick, Cornelius, Claudius, Julius and
Octavius, but, with the exception of the first, they were given
very little education and, at a quite early age, taken out by their
father to hunt for smugglers. Frederick did succeed as a private
schoolmaster but the rest of the boys died young. Burdened with
such a family, James Miles must have longed for his daughter to
effect a match with someone more affluent than a lawyer's clerk.

William Barnes was always the least mercenary of men and,
from his point of view the response of Julia's parents was an unfair
one. Clearly they did not appreciate his true worth or the depth of
his attachment to their daughter. His sense of injured merit would
have luxuriated indignantly with Samuel Johnson's dictum: 'Slow
rises worth by poverty deprest', but his natural response was to
try to prove the worth rather than to alleviate the poverty, and he
attempted the former by writing a poem.

This first published piece appeared in the *Weekly Entertainer*
in 1820. It is called *To Julia*:

> When the moonlight is spread on these meadows so green,
>   Which the Frome's limpid current glides by,
> To mark its calm progress, to gaze on the scene,
>   May delight the poetical eye.
>
> To one who in some remote climate has pass'd
>   A long absence from all he lov'd here,
> How sweet the first glance of the land, as at last
>   To his own native Isle he draws near.

But by far more delightful and sweet 'tis to gaze
  On thy bright azure eyes, as they dart
From under those tremulous lids their bright rays
  And glances for glances impart.

The smile of the muse may the poet beguile,
  Or the smile of gay nature in spring;
To others dame fortune's precarious smile,
  Its many enjoyments may bring.

I would envy no poet with thy smile if blest,
  Nor at fortune's dire frown e'er repine;
For muse's or fortune's smile ne'er yet possess'd
  Ought to rival the sweetness of thine.[5]

Lucy Baxter is unintentionally right; this is 'poesy' rather than
poetry, the 'eye' referred to in the poem is poetical rather than
poetic. The poem is little more than a ritual gesturing, a succession of stock poetic sentiments from the eighteenth century
cobbled together by clumsy inversions and the employment of
'tises', 'e'ers' and 'oughts' at crucial moments. Eyes, in such
poems always 'dart' their rays and lids are always 'tremulous'.
Yet before we smile at the plagiaristic gaucheness of this poem
we would do well to recollect that it is the composition of an
eighteen-year-old youth of practically no formal education. The
achievement here must be measured against the challenge. Even
in this first poem, however, which will serve as a yardstick by
which to measure his later education in poetry, there is a hint of a
certain technical facility which, if developed and brought to bear
upon a genuine perception, would achieve much.

To Julia was followed by a number of other poems in the Weekly
Entertainer and, in 1820, ten poems were collected in a little paper
book with a title page which read: Poetical Pieces by William
Barnes, Dorchester, Printed by G Clark, High Street, MDCCCXX.
The poems included were: Destiny, The Farewell, On Woman's
Love, The Home of my Heart, Lines, Though You Smile at my Zeal,
The Death of Adults, To Julia, Danger, and Faithful Isabel. Every
poem in some way supplies an oblique commentary upon his
relationship with Julia and it must be admitted that the volume

has more autobiographical than artistic interest. The most in-
flammatory of all the poems is *Destiny*, the first verse of which
reads:

> Her fortunate stars had to Julia given,
>   Of lovers a numerous train,
> Who for twelve months, or more, had incessantly striven
>   To win her fair hand – but in vain.
> They were all youths of merit, although they were poor,
>   And to one she'd nigh given her heart;
> But her father he lik'd the pecun'ary ore,
> Insomuch that in one of his passions he swore
> That Julia should ne'er again enter his door,
>   If to him she her hand should impart.[6]

Quite what effect Barnes expected this poem to have is not
certain, but the identity of the fictional 'Julia' would have been
no mystery in the small county town and James Camford Miles
must have provoked many a hidden smirk when his alleged love
for the 'pecun'ary ore' was discussed by his contemporaries. Far
from winning him over, the poem further inflamed his temper at
the sight of his daughter's suitor. Mrs Miles was presented in a
light which was no more flattering:

> Her mama urged with much assiduity too,
>   When she thought of becoming a wife,
> The advantage of keeping the maxim in view,
>   That 'gold's the best passport thro' life.'[7]

The poem goes on to extol the worthiness of 'Cyprian', the
earnest young lover who clearly stands for Barnes himself.
'Julia's' mother seems to have rather confused views on life for,
despite her recommendation of the pecuniary principle above all
others, she also advises her daughter that marriages are really a
matter of fate. Julia then meets a gypsy in a wood who gives her a
description of the man she is to marry, one which provides the
reader with a clue to how the youthful Barnes liked to think of
himself:

> He is rather genteel, his complexion is light,
> His eyes *are* rather dark, and his hair black as night,
> And I certainly think that his love should requite,
>   Were it not for my father's restriction.[8]

The upshot of the poem is that Julia determines to follow the voice of 'Destiny' and to marry Cyprian whose 'industry' will 'partly supply' the witholding of her father's gold. It is worth noting that this rather naïve little poem, written in early manhood, proclaims many of the convictions which shaped Barnes's mature life, his determination to overcome the defects of birth and fortune by a life of industry and undoubted moral worth.

The poems that follow dramatise a variety of relationships with fictional heroines: the poet cannot live without his Eliza; Emily believes that happiness flows only from splendour and riches while Isabel, by contrast, dies at the absence of her beloved Cyprian; Anna resides beneath the green canopy of leaves on the margin of the Frome and, because of that, the place will be for ever the 'Home' of the poet's 'Heart'. *Poetical Pieces* enabled Barnes to advertise his burgeoning scholarship to the town. The book includes epigraphs from Pope and Virgil and an appropriate elegy on the death of Adonis, a god who fills a suitable role as a young man, despised in love, now mourned by Venus. The book seemed to its youthful author as printed evidence of his sincerity and rightful sense of injured merit. It is doubtful if Mr Miles took the point.

In 1822 the young poet published a far more ambitious work, the title-page of which reads: *Orra: A Lapland Tale by William Barnes, Dorchester: Printed by J. Criswick, High West Street, 1822*. A copy of the poem kept at the County Museum bears the handwritten inscription 'The 1st Poem ever published'. If the handwriting is by Barnes, and it looks as if it is, then it is yet another instance of the selective memory of his old age which, in this case, has quite forgotten the *Poetical Pieces*. The Museum also possesses a manuscript of the poem in a mottled-covered exercise book; the handwriting is bold and elegant as one would expect of a man who lived by the art of calligraphy. It is probably the very copy sent to Criswick for printing.

Orra is a much more extensive work than anything he had previously attempted. It is a narrative poem of sixty-five stanzas each of eight lines and cast in tetrameters, with rhyme-schemes of ababcdcd. It's scholarly origins are proclaimed by epigraphs from Virgil and Dryden and an apparatus of notes at the end. Barnes took his colouring from Acerbi's account of his voyage through Lapland in 1798-9. Despite the exotic location, however, the story is the now familiar one of true love blighted by parental opposition.

The story is a melodramatic one. The scene is set in a land where the 'solitary coast/Looks out upon the frozen Arctic sea'. Orra, a young Lapland maid is visited and courted by 'young Lawo', a mountain Lap, while her father gives a feast to his friends of the maritime tribes. The conversation of the young lovers is interrupted by Orra's father who demands to know the identity of his daughter's visitor. Lawo confesses his mountain origins and declares that he has now left his roving tribe to come to claim Orra's hand. In lines that might have described Barnes's first vision of Julia, he tells of his previous meetings with Orra:

> As graceful as the silvery cloud
>   That glides upon the summer air,
> She moved, a monarch might be proud,
>   The love of such a form to share;
>   I marked her shape, her flowing hair,
> And eyes of bright ethereal blue,
>   And Oh! I thought, a form so fair
> The liveliest fancy never drew.[9]

Lawo asks Orra's father to pledge their love in a ceremonial cup of wine but the old man refuses and informs him that even now Lawo's rival is enjoying accepted wine in the adjacent tent. This rival is unnamed but we are told that he possesses deer 'thick as the stars in heaven' and many boats and sledges, all which booty, presumably, comprises the Laplandic equivalent of 'pecun'ary ore'. Unlike Barnes, Lawo is the sort who gives up quickly. He gives one sigh and spreads his sail. When he fails to return in due season, Orra goes in search of him. She takes a little boat and makes her way through mountainous waves to a barren island he is known to frequent. She is forced to take shelter in a cave and, when she wakes in the morning, she finds that her boat is being swept out to sea by the tempest. She is condemned to death either by starvation on the island or by drowning in vain atempts to get off it. Barnes does not actually depict her death but is content to leave her in melodramatic extremity.

That *Orra* is an impressive technical performance for so young

a man may best be illustrated by two stanzas from the Introduction:

> There in the fleet Pulkha, along the plain
>   They glide, exulting in the rein-deer's speed,
> Nor dream of happier regions, where the rein
>   Controuls the gallant and the mighty steed,
>   Where flocks around the verdant mountains feed,
> And yellow corn embrowns the fading year.
>   Nor are they less content, than those who lead
> A life of luxury and splendour here.
>
> Warm glows their summer, while the sky displays
>   The solar orb, but soon the summer flies;
> The wintry air soon chills the short'ning days,
>   And suddenly the blasted verdure dies;
>   Then gathering clouds, and wintry storms arise,
> And the pale sun withdraws his feeble light,
>   No longer striving with the gloomy skies,
> But leaves the land to winter and to night.[10]

The diction here is again drawn from stock eighteenth century
epithets – 'gallant and mighty steed', 'verdant mountains', 'solar
orb' – and the moralising about those who lead lives of luxury and
splendour looks to be little more than conventional gesture. Yet all
poets learn by plagiarism, a poetic tradition needs to be absorbed
before it can be surpassed. In *Orra* Barnes is at the plagiarising
stage; there are echoes here of Pope, Collins and Cowper while the
last line quoted sounds like something from Gray's *Elegy*. There
are, however, small triumphs to record, such lines as 'And yellow
corn embrowns the fading year'. The poem gives a fair indication
of the extent of the poet's reading and also of his growing skill in
handling both verse form and the pastoral convention. At least
one critic thought highly of *Orra* for, after its publication, Barnes
received an anonymous letter which greeted him as 'The Poet
Laureate of Dorchester' and celebrated his merits in seven verses,
the first of which ran:

> Barnes, when thy muse inspires the song
>   My soul is all on fire,
> The numbers sweetly flow along
>   While I well pleased admire.[11]

Unfortunately the quality of the writing cannot have reinforced
the poet's confidence in his critic.

In his first years in Dorchester, William Barnes began to develop a number of interests which were to remain with him for a
lifetime. His eye was not merely 'poetical' but artistic as well.
The publication of *Orra* was paid for by the engraving of wooden
blocks to illustrate Criswick's own book, *A Walk Round Dorchester*. The 1820 edition of the book contained only one plate, a
rather indistinct view of the town with Fordington. In 1822 a new
edition appeared with eight wood engravings by Barnes. They
were of Lulworth Castle, Milton Abbey, Cerne Abbey, the
Roman amphitheatre at Dorchester, Bindon Abbey, Corfe
Castle, Durdle Door and Poundbury.

Wood engraving became a serious pursuit for Barnes, so much
so that, at times, he thought of taking it up as a profession. Both
his early books of poems are illustrated by small engravings. The
first poem in *Poetical Pieces*, *Destiny*, is embellished by a figure
crouched over a fire, presumably a representation of the gypsy
mentioned in the poem. The book contains two other figures,
that of a cupid upon a fiery podium and another of a figure with
chords of a musical instrument, the latter figure meant, perhaps,
to represent the Muse. In a monograph upon Barnes's engravings, Vere L. Oliver offers the view that the engravings to
Poetical Pieces are not by Barnes, but the argument is against him
both on grounds of style and probability.[12] We know that Barnes
engraved the illustrations to *Orra* for the title page informs us of
the fact. The text of the book contains three figures: a man seated
in a boat with oars and sails; a cupid with stretched bow; a
female figure, presumably meant to be Orra, dressed in volumi-
nous skirt and habit, gazing into the sea with two icebergs in the
background. The figure of this last is not well done and the facial
expression which was surely intended to depict pathos succeeds
in being merely distorted.

Barnes appended an advertisement to *Orra* which clearly indicates that he was considering the visual arts as his possible way
to a new career and to advancement. The advertisement is headed by an engraving of a larger block, depicting two figures,
apparently both female and dressed in Roman clothes, gazing
out of a window or possibly at the decorated panelling of a wall.
The wording of the advertisement runs as follows:

'The Author of this poem having taught himself the arts of Copper and Wood Engraving and Drawing, takes this opportunity of informing his readers, that he will feel very grateful for any Orders they may please to honour him with in the Profession of an Engraver, etc., and assures them, he will spare no pains which will enable him to execute them with elegance.

Visiting Cards, Bill-heads, etc. Engraved on Copper, in every variety of style. Ornamental Designs for Printers on Wood.

Likenesses taken in Pencil, at from 7s.6d to 10s.6d each; and correct Drawings made of Antiquities, Architecture, Curiosities, etc.'

No doubt the intention behind the advertisement was initially to supplement his income as an engrossing clerk and thus to persuade James Miles that he had a sufficient income to marry his daughter. Nevertheless, it suggests that Barnes was beginning to think of himself as an engraver. 'About the same time, he wrote later, I cut a few other blocks for Mr Criswick, Mr Clark and others, as pieces for bill-heads or hand-bills; or catalogues and tracts, and spent most if not all the money which they brought me in boks, though I soon tried my hand at copper plate engraving and cypher cutting, and for some months before I went to Mere, I kept myself by engraving, drawing and engrossing law documents.'[13]

So serious was he that, in 1822, he allowed some friends to write on his behalf to London, with the intention of asking a professional engraver to take him as an articled apprentice. Replies were received from Edward Scriven, the eminent engraver, and also from E. Walton on behalf of Rudolph Ackerman, the fine-art publisher in the Strand. Scriven replied that Barnes's work demonstrated 'evident signs of a marked talent for the arts' but pointed out that it was impossible for the artist to expect to earn a tolerable salary immediately, and that he could hardly expect to be paid while learning. Walton (for Ackermann) acknowledged the receipt of some drawings and engravings and remarked upon the 'considerable show of talent in his performance' but also concluded that the young artist could never hope to arrive at that degree of eminence which would ensure respectability in the profession until he had undergone professional training.[14]

For the moment, Barnes's dream of becoming a professional

artist and engraver were forced into abeyance. It did not entirely die, however, and for the next thirteen years he continued to practise engraving in his spare moments. While at Mere he cut blocks advertising himself as an engraver in copper and wood living variously at Mere, Dorchester and Bath. It was also at Mere that he purchased and used 'a very small and pretty copper plate press'. His work consisted largely of depictions of ancient buildings and objects of interest such as Napper's Mite in Dorchester, the pulpit of Nailsea church and Henry Fielding's house at East Stour. His representations of the human figure are often clumsy but his views of churches and old houses are often very effective. A number of his blocks were used to illustrate local guide books and others were cut especially to illustrate his antiquarian articles in *The Gentleman's Magazine*. He seems to have given up engraving round about 1844, probably because his duties as a schoolmaster and his new-found interest in the writing of poetry left him little time for the art. In that year he was also seeking both graduation and ordination and he may have thought that such a manual trade as engraving might be considered ungentlemanly by the parents of his pupils. Another reason for his abandonment of engraving may have been the rheumatism of the hands which eventually impaired his fine handwriting. Nevertheless, in his career as an amateur engraver, he produced at least 190 blocks and his best work has been compared to that of his great contemporary, Bewick.

In 1822 he and Julia were betrothed, but his prospects were still no better than when he had first joined Coombs some four years before. What he desperately needed was a profession which would enable him to keep his future wife and children in a respectable way. Furthermore, it needed to be one which required no capital, no professional training, and which could be entered into at once. Engraving was clearly not the answer. One day a chance presented itself. William Carey received a letter from Mere, in Wiltshire, informing him that his old schoolmaster, Mr Robertson, had died, and that there was no one to take his place. The idea came quite suddenly to Carey. Why should not William Barnes go to Mere to become a schoolmaster?

3
The Idyll, Mere
1823-1835

There were agonised discussions between William Barnes and
Julia on whether or not he should take up Carey's suggestion and
go to Mere. Though the town was just over the Wiltshire border,
communications with Dorchester were difficult and his removal
would separate them for many months at a time. Even when he
found time to visit Julia, her father would probably not receive
him and would certainly not welcome him as a guest. Furthermore, Gilbert Carey's blithe assumption that his friend could
simply take over Robertson's school was an extremely dubious
one. In effect, the school had died with the master. All that
Barnes knew for sure was that there was now an opening for a
school at Mere. The temptations to remain in Dorchester with
Julia were great, especially when sustained by the thought that
one day, of course, he would depart, to go to Bath or London to
make his fortune as an artist or engraver.

It was Julia who rejected such romantic dreams and also the
temptation to do nothing. Though only eighteen years of age she
then began to display the tenacity of purpose that distinguished
her maturity. She pointed out that, if Barnes were to remain in
Dorchester, they would never be married, for he would never
earn sufficient money as a lawyer's clerk to satisfy her father that
he could support a family. He must better his prospects. Besides,
they both knew that, however kind Mr Coombs may have been
to him, the drudgery of copying out legal documents all day was
far below his talents. He needed a profession which would allow
him to rise in the world and support a family in something like
gentility. She argued passionately, and Barnes was both charmed
and won over. In truth his real reservation was one that he could
not utter; that she might forget him in his absence and choose a
richer suitor, as her father wished. Yet how could he think such

thoughts when her lovely earnestness of manner was coupled with such a practical regard for their future together? He agreed. He would go to Mere.

He bade goodbye to Coombs, Carey and all his Dorchester friends in the dark winter days of 1822 and, in the New Year, arrived at the Talbot Inn in Mere. While they handed his box down from the coach, he looked around him and found a very drab town indeed, consisting chiefly of small grey stone houses, with bow windows, with a few inns round the square and a mill at the bottom of the town. He soon found lodgings in Salisbury Street and he was to remain in lodgings for the next four years before Julia married him in 1827. It was a lonely existence, and one that tested his resolution to the utmost but, in so doing, fostered in him those habits of self-help and of scholarly pursuits that were to remain with him for the rest of his life.

Having settled in, he began at once to make enquiries about Robertson's school. His worst fears were realised, for that school had simply ceased to exist. As a completely untrained master, with no experience, he was now faced with the task of starting a school by finding premises and attracting scholars. The former was not a great problem for he was able to rent Robertson's schoolroom in the Old Cross Loft above the mediaeval market place. Mere had been a market town since 1408, when Henry iv had granted it a charter, but the agricultural decline following the end of the Napoleonic Wars had much diminished trade. Now the market consisted chiefly of stalls which projected from the building in which Barnes held his school. The Market House had immense gothic windows and doorways fitted with wooden doors. On market days, these doors were opened and the stalls pushed out into the street. Barnes's scholars had to climb up a small staircase to the schoolroom above, which also housed the town clock. Thus his first lessons were often drowned by the hubbub of buying and selling from the market below, and his remarks were punctuated throughout by the ticking of the ancient mechanism. The room was a commodious one, however, for it had served as the court house of the Duchy of Cornwall for over four centuries and, even in Barnes's time, made do in the evenings as the town's theatre.[1]

It was much more difficult to recruit scholars, especially as there was little money in the town. Barnes was obliged to walk the drab late-winter streets to call upon shopkeepers and trades-men of whom it had been reported that they might be willing to send their sons to his new school. Then he was obliged to haggle with prospective parents who were only too keen to persuade him to make special discounts in favour of their own sons for real or imagined reasons. Barnes lacked the commercial instinct, and this routine of public importunity and frequent rejection was deeply distasteful to his retiring nature. Yet he stuck it out and, by 16 April, he was able to write to Julia to tell her that he now had ten pupils. He had, he explained, not written before, be-cause he did not wish to do so until he had some good news for her.

During his year as a schoolmaster at Mere, Barnes placed a series of advertisements in the local newspapers to attract pupils. At first he tended to emphasise the classical language which he could offer but subsequently his advertisements stressed the commercial advantage to be gained. By 17 May 1823 he had twelve pupils and, on 12 August, he was able to write to tell Julia that he had no fewer than twenty-four. Unfortunately he was obliged to add the fact that he could not obtain his 'regular charge for the whole of them'. Parents who had sent their boys to him in the previous term would not always pay their bills in full; others demanded rebates because their boys had absented them-selves during haymaking. Some parents simply took advantage of the inexperienced young schoolmaster, while others, no doubt, genuinely found it difficult to survive in farming or business and could not find the money. One of Barnes's prob-lems was that his fees were retrospective. The other was that he needed a commercially-minded partner; this lack he supplied when he married Julia who, from then on, conducted the busi-ness side of his affairs.

He took as pupils boys between the ages of six and fifteen, most of whom were the sons of farmers, shopkeepers and profes-sional people. Their parents expected them to be given a practical education of real use in difficult times. In the classroom Barnes was expected to give attention to reading and writing commercial documents, and also to arithmetical problems of profit and loss and the calculation of areas of land. Parents were little interested in Barnes's talents as a teacher of Latin and classical literature. Those first weeks of his career as schoolmaster were spent in teaching by day and paying calls upon non-payers or prospective customers in the evenings. When he retired to his lodgings for a solitary evening meal he was often exhausted and, in November he wrote to Julia to declare that 'The function of a schoolmaster is certainly laborious. I find myself generally fatigued in body and mind in the evening.'

As spring came on, he was more able to take walks round the town. An April evening stroll would take him from the Market House which stood in the Square, up to the Talbot Inn where, perhaps, a team of horses were bringing the London Mail to a clattering halt. The little town had only recently received a much-needed boost to its economy by being selected to serve as a staging post for the newly-developing coach service between London and Exeter. Social life in the town centred round its inns, two of which were of some antiquity. Barnes rarely visited the Ship Inn, for it would not have been considered proper for a young schoolmaster to be seen in a place noted for low company and cock-fighting. The Talbot, however, or the 'Old George' as it was sometimes called, might serve as a venue to meet a parent bringing his son into Mere for the first time. Besides, the anti-quarian which now was stirring in Barnes liked to hear of the associations of that old inn with Charles ii. Apparently, when the King was on the run and going about the country incognito, he had lunched at the Talbot. The landlord was a loyalist but a cautious man; he had enquired of his guest as to whether he was 'a friend to Caesar' and, on hearing that he was, had induced the still-disguised king to drink a health to himself.[2]

On summer evenings Barnes was able to wander farther afield. To the north-west of the town stood Castle Hill with its mys-terious ruined walls that had been built by Henry iii. From the summit of the Hill he could look down from the primrose banks to the people walking Salisbury Street below him. As he gazed south he could glimpse the wooded country of Blackmore Vale ten miles away and the blue outlines of the Dorset hills beyond. Those hills masked the spire of St Peter's at Dorchester where, perhaps, even now, his Julia was walking up Cornhill. Some-times he visited the parish church of St Michael the Archangel where he would sit and sketch the beautiful 15th century wooden screen or ruminate upon the life of Sir John Bettesthorne, who founded the chantry chapel and whose image was depicted in brass upon the stone pavement. Sometimes he walked out behind the church to look at the old Chantry House. It had belonged to the Grove family, friends of Charles II. He thought wistfully of the pleasure it would be to welcome Julia as his bride to so lovely a house.

He was a lonely young man, for his heart was thirty miles away in Dorchester. There was possible company for him among the young men who gathered at the Talbot but he was too abstemious and high-principled to desire that kind of company. One parent, Charles Card, was friendly and helpful from the first but, though Barnes was grateful for frequent favours from a man who was the town's largest provision merchant, this was not really the kind of company to satisfy him. There was little chance of meeting a young man as cultivated as Edward Fuller. Henry Wake, the Rector of St Michael's, was rather arrogant and not at all like Lane Fox and Richman. Barnes had to accept that Mere was no county town like Dorchester. There were no country gentry to promote even a limited level of provincial learning, and he had to rely upon himself for cultural diversion.

Night after night the young man sat alone after supper with little to occupy his mind save thoughts of Julia or of home. He wrote to Julia to inform her that his principal 'pursuit out of school (was) poetry' of which he had 'written several pieces lately'. He had begun to teach himself Italian and his poetry was chiefly modelled on the sonnets of Petrarch. He was a linguist of great application and facility and soon commenced a programme of studies which still impresses when one considers the sparsity of his books. Years later he noted in his scrapbook:

'At Mere I did my best in my spare time for improvement in scholarship, and took up in turn Latin, Greek, French, Italian and German. I began Persian with Lees Grammar and for a little time Russian which being wanting of old lore I soon cast aside.'

It seemed to him that success in his new profession would be determined by his own fitness for the task and, therefore, the arduous programme of reading that he set himself, by the flickering candlelight in his drab lodgings, was not merely a solace and a diversion but the way to professional success and to the winning of Julia. A more commercially-minded friend might have advised him that he would do better to ingratiate himself to the trades-men of the town at the Talbot. His studies were not always solitary and, when he met someone who could teach him a language, he took full advantage of the situation. M. Masson, for example, was an old prisoner-of-war from Napoleonic times, who had stayed on in Mere and married an Englishwoman. He was willing to teach Barnes French, no doubt in return for favours of some kind.

Barnes may be considered a little over-earnest in his search for knowledge, but it must be remembered with what few resources he had started his self-education and how precarious was his professional success. For these reasons he would often moralise both to Julia and himself. He wrote to his sweetheart to declare that: 'I know that industry and virtue are the grand sources of human happiness and that they are valuable qualities in a female, and such a proof of your possessing them must of course be agreeable to me.' For she too had taken employment as a teacher to prepare herself to be his helpmate. He addressed himself in one of his recently-written sonnets:

> 'O carpe diem! wisdom health and strength
> Were not bestowed upon us here to waste
>   In mental lethargy or sensual joy.
> Tear vices from thy bosom, ere at length
> Thou findest them too strong to be displaced,
> And give thy faculties their full employ.'[3]

In truth the vices to be torn from his bosom were almost entirely imaginary. His nights alone are best captured in a brief note he added to a letter to Julia: 'I am writing this letter in my room where I have spent many a studious hour and am accom-panied only by my little dog which is amusing himself by en-deavouring to catch the shadows thrown by the candle by which I am writing. May heaven grant that my efforts to obtain happi-ness may not be as vain.'

It must have seemed all the more galling for him to receive a facetious letter from his old friend Mr Jacob, a Dorchester book-seller. After providing his friend with a brief account of the delights of the London theatres and with Kean's portrayal of Shylock, Jacob added:

'a propos – how is your heart affected, is there any fair one at Mere, that bids for it, is there any that is likely to make you forget your allegiance to the fair Julia, I know your heart is made of very *malleable* material and I think it is dangerous – but in Poetry all is fair, to Poets all is lovely.'

Such levity must have seemed cruelly out of place to the faithful young schoolmaser poring over the letter alone in his room. Yet, despite Barnes's lifelong attachment to Julia, Jacob may have truly grasped that his friend was always just a little susceptible to women, especially young ones.

Throughout the four years of their separation, Barnes and Julia kept up a fairly regular correspondence.[4] Barnes's letters were written in his beautiful regular hand, the ink now yellowed with age; he was always affectionate and straightforward. His earlier letters tend, at times, to a gentle melancholia, but the tone becomes more assured and cheerful as he became settled in Mere society. At times he apologised for having nothing to say and filled out the page with a poem written specially for Julia. Her letters were more formal; the first is addressed to her 'Dear Friend' but thereafter, until the eve of their marriage, she began each one 'Dear Barnes'. The formality may have derived from her conceptions of propriety or, perhaps, even at that time, she did not wish to compromise herself too much on paper.

Her first letter, written in the spring of 1823, announced an important change in their situation brought about by a change of heart in her father:

On Tuesday I went for a little ride out of town with my Father and as we were returning in the evening he began a conversation which I have long wished to hear him begin. It was, as you may suppose, concerning us. He told me plainly he had no objection to you in the least – but on the contrary you were a young person whom he much respected. But then he told me that when you first walked with me I was but a mere child and it was his duty as an affectionate father to make objections. But still he wished me to understand that he would not be an obstacle in the way I had placed my affections, by no means. He thought your intentions were Honourable – but at the same time you had not openly avowed them to him and he should by no means give his consent to anything until you had. I then reminded him that you had written twice and come twice to the house with the intention to speak with him on the subject.

He said that he was aware of that but still, whenever he met you in the street you always passed him with such contempt that he certainly did not like it but he thought if he had but half an hour's conversation with you that would set you to rights and you would be very good friends. But to conclude this subject, he said if I choose I may let you know what he said which I certainly thought best.

This relaxation in the hostility of James Cameron Miles meant that their relationship was now a recognised one. From then on, Barnes was accepted as a visitor and holiday guest to the Miles' home in Dorchester and also to Nailsea, after the family had removed there in 1825. Without this lifting of the embargo it would have been very difficult for the young lovers to have met at all.

Julia's letters are a curious compound of sincerity, archness and moralising. In counselling patience in her lover she reminds him that: 'We should ever remember that patience is required in everything we undertake' and, when recounting the tale of the dreadful storms and floods that struck Dorchester and Weymouth in November 1824, she observes to her lover that: 'When we recount the misfortunes of our fellow creatures how thankful we ought to be that we are spared the many trials and afflictions which so many experience.' In this last letter she had to tell him the distressing news of the death of his old patron, Henry Richman, who had been killed with his wife when a stack of chimneys had crashed through their roof. The grief of a friend must have been partly assuaged by the delight of a lover to find a humble little note at the conclusion of the letter: 'Excuse the imperfections I am sure they are numerous.' Even Julia was beginning to regard him as a schoolmaster!

There are signs in her letters that she was beginning to be aware that his developing erudition was taking him into fields where she could not follow. For his part, he began to explain things to her rather too much. There was a risk that he might have turned into a prig had it not been for his infectious sense of humour. He liked to compare himself to his favourite poet, Petrarch, whose story he recounted to Julia in a letter dated 4 December 1826:

about the same time I translated for amusement one of the Sonnets of Petrarch, an Italian poet who lived about 400 years ago and who is celebrated for the sweetness of his verses, and for his attachment to the amiable Laura. As I thought it suited my case at the time in some points I have sent it to you for your amusement and I may add that if I resembled him as much in my poetry as in my attachment to my mistress I might expect immortal fame. Another Italian writer in speaking of the excellence of his verses, says 'Quanto eggli tocca si cangia in auro': 'Whatever he touched he turned to gold.' Happy for Petrarch if this had been literally instead of figuratively true, for then he might not have seen, as he did, his Laura married to a richer rival.

Clearly, the dread that Julia would forsake him was still there.

The major change in their lives in these years was the move of the Miles family to Nailsea, Somerset, in the summer of 1825. James Miles did not wish to leave Dorchester and petitioned against it, but as an officer of the Customs and Excise he had to go where he was bid, and the family left the town in April. For the young lovers, the chief anxiety in this was that their separation would be yet more prolonged and their meetings more infrequent. Dorchester was dear to them by old association and Nailsea was reported to be a dirty place where a constant wind blew smuts from the largest glass manufactuary in the country. Their fears were exaggerated, however, and Barnes soon spent the first of a number of happy holidays at Nailsea. While exploring Somerset he made a series of sketches for his wood engravings of local antiquities. Julia had initially remained in Dorchester, to carry on teaching, but she joined the family in November 1825. Almost immediately she was very ill and Barnes was frantic about her health. Later, while holidaying with the family in Somerset, a moment's weakness exhibited by Julia on a walk provoked a Petrarchan sonnet from him:

CLIMBING NAILSEA HILL

When thou didst try to climb that arduous hill
    That rises steeply from thy dear abode,
Because thou wert so feeble and so ill
    Thou turnedst back from that long upward road;
    And there were things, in that sad hour, that shew'd
How griev'd thou wert to find thyself so weak,
    For bitter tears upon thy bosom flow'd,
Although thou wert too feeble, then, to speak.

I know thy gentle soul is bound for heaven:-
    But in some future illness should it yearn
    From this terrestrial vale to take its flight,

Thus may it be, that ere it may be riven
   From that sweet form, it may again return,
   Still, still, to give this lower world delight.[5]

In October 1826 Barnes wrote to Julia to give her a report on the
progress of his enterprise but made it plain that he was still
toying with the thought of another profession altogether: 'My
school is somewhat improved but I am not at all satisfied with it
at present and I cannot tell whether January will find me a
Schoolmaster or an artist.' By December he had applied for a post
as third master in 'a large Classical and Mathematical School' at
Plymouth, but had failed in his attempt. Ironically, the successful candidate had been preferred because he was a married man
and, therefore, able to accept boarders into his house. Barnes
had, by this time, come to believe that the taking of boarders
would be the way to expand his own school, but to do so he
needed a wife, and to secure her, he needed suitable premises.
On March 21 1827, he was able to write to her with the news for
which they had both been waiting. He had been offered a lease
on Chantry House itself:

My Dear Julia,
   The large house is offered to me at 20 guineas per ann. and considering
its size and convenience I do not think it dear. It has 6 or 7 rooms above
stairs, a large Dining Room with a Parlour, Kitchens etc below and all
grates, furnaces etc. are remaining. The Taxes are to be paid by the
tenant but the garden may be considered as a drawback ...
   The house stands in a private situation which is so much the better
and it has a Play Ground. You will doubtless see by the tone of my letter
that I am now actuated by views of self-interest as well as a desire to give
you information with regard to the state of the affair but as I hope my
interest will be ultimately yours, I hope you will forgive me.
   With regards to the family, I remain
         Yours sincerely
         W. Barnes

   In such an extensive property they could keep two schools, one
for boys and one for girls, and, even more importantly, he could
take boarders. Indeed, in this same letter to Julia, Barnes took the
opportunity of discreetly enquiring whether James Cameron
Miles might be willing to send his son Octavius to Mere, as a
boarder, the following midsummer. The decision on Chantry

House was quickly made. They were to be married at Nailsea in the summer holidays and were to take the lease on the property in order to open their schools.

Barnes's four years as a solitary schoolmaster had not only developed a strain of self-reliance in him, they had also confirmed his rather withdrawn and scholarly nature. He had become a compulsive reader and a young man given to brooding and day-dreams. So much of his time had been spent alone in his room, thinking of Julia, recollecting the holidays spent with her or anticipating their next meeting. It was those holidays which provided the material of much of his early poetry. He wrote a poem about Maumbury Ring, the amphitheatre in Dorchester, where he was wont to walk with her[6] and another about their boat excursions upon the Frome:

> And Julia sitting at the stern,
> Looks on me with a winning smile,
> And gently asks me to return.
> I turn the boat; the stream is wide,
> And we are sailing with the tide
> And throwing down the oars to rest
> I sit me down by Julia's side
> And press her to my breast.[7]

By 22 June 1827 Barnes had taken out a lease on Chantry House and felt that he was at last in a position to write formally to James Miles about his wish to marry Julia. In the letter he proudly announced that he had taken a 'commodious house in Mere' in which, with Julia's assistance, he intended to open 'a Boarding School and seminary for Young Ladies'. He reminded Miles that his attachment to Julia had been formed in 'extreme youth' and had survived an 'absence of considerable duration'. (It was, in fact, nine years since he had first seen her descending from a coach in High West Street, Dorchester, and their engagement had been a very protracted one by the standards of the day.) He concluded by informing his future father-in-law that, should the school at Mere fail, then his 'dernier ressort' would be 'the more pleasing occupation of the Graver', or he would return to Dorchester as a teacher of art and modern languages.

Inevitably, marriage ended the long correspondence between the lovers. Barnes's last letters are an odd mixture of the romantic and the practical. He tells her of the details of the house and of the purchases they need to make to furnish it. His very last letter, written in May 1827, includes a list of the costs of mattresses, counterpanes and ticking as supplied by his good friend, Mr Card, of Mere. When the summer holidays came round he departed at once for Nailsea, where he and Julia were married at the parish church on 9 July. Years later he recorded the event in his scrapbook in an entry which combines the tones of a lover and of a young professional: 'In 1827 I took Chantry House at Mere, and brought home my most loveworthy and ever beloved wife Julia Miles and then took boarders.'

Then began an idyllic domestic life, which he was to celebrate years later in the best-known of all his poems, *My Orcha'd in Linden Lea*. He and Julia lived an entirely private life at the Chantry – or as private as it could be with boys boarding in the house and scholars of both sexes arriving at the door every morning for their lessons. Barnes may not have been the first poet to live at the Chantry for, in 1530, Wynken de Worde, an assistant of Caxton's printed a poem entitled the *Fantasy of the Fox* which was reputed to have been written by a priest in the house. The Chantry was probably about a hundred years old at the time, for, in 1425, Henry VI had authorised that a piece of land should be set aside for its building.[8]

The exterior of the house shows a rectangular building of grey stone with stone-walled gardens. It stands so close to St Michael's Church that it looks, from the south, as if the church tower is projecting from the roof of the Chantry. Between the house and the church are the small gardens in one of which Barnes loved to train his peaches and espaliers and another of which served as his school playground. He even had his own private path out of the Chantry to a small door in St Michael's southern front. The interior of the house has been much changed but, in Barnes's day, it acquired some of the nineteenth century clutter of plastering, wooden dados, partitions and iron grates that have since been removed. On the ground floor the Great Hall of mediaeval times was probably his schoolroom with the family parlour beyond. Julia had her kitchen in the eastern wing and the boys' bedrooms were directly above this. In the small coach house outside, Barnes set up a copper press which Mr Card bought for him in London.

Much as he learned to love the house, it was the garden which specially pleased him. Far from being a 'drawback' as he had feared, it became his delight. There was a lawn which ran down to a lake with a small waterfall, fish, fowl, a yew tree and, if 'Linden Lea' is to be believed, an apple tree leaning low. The rank of elms at the bottom of the garden is now gone, but the lake is still there as are the waterfall and the great spreading yew tree. The name of his most famous poem remains something of a mystery; a 'lea' is a tract of open ground or grassland such as the lawn at the Chantry, but there is no record of 'lindens' or lime trees in the garden, though a young line of them shades the visitor to the north door of St Michael's and may have replaced others from Barnes's time. It may be, however, that he simply chose the phrase 'Linden Lea' because he liked the alliterative fall of the words. Whatever the truth, it is certain that the garden afforded the busy schoolmaster a contemplative delight in natural beauty as he tended his peaches and scythed the grass on the lea.

Family and boarders began the day with a simple breakfast of bread and milk, followed by morning prayers and then lessons which started at nine. Barnes usually began by giving the whole school a piece of dictation and then by expatiating upon the sentences so as to make them more meaningful. Julia simultaneously conducted her 'seminary' for young ladies in another room and she may have taken the youngest boys as well. Throughout the morning, Barnes would supervise groups of boys with their slates until it was time to take lunch with the boarders in the kitchen. The afternoon was spent in rather more informal studies, for Barnes loved to take his scholars for walks in the countryside so that they might be taught to identify plants, trees, and animals. After tea the boys were set an evening task to complete and then the day boys went home while the boarders, in summer, went out into the playground, or clustered round the fire on winter nights. Long before he could afford an usher, Barnes learned to keep half an eye on his charges while he practised with his lathe or fiddle or wrote his poetry.

For six years, until her mother joined her to help in the house, Julia had sole charge of the kitchen, the house and the girls' school. Many a time while supervising her charges she would have to break off to attend to a parent or tradesman who had come to call. She also had to attend to shopping and canvassing for more pupils, for Barnes disliked going out into the streets of Mere – indeed, in the early years of married life he became something of a recluse. On her arrival Julia had taken over the business of the school and it was she who provided the necessary practical complement to Barnes's pedagogic talents to ensure that their various schools were financially successful.

Such a load of work was an onerous one for a young woman, and was increased by the births of three children during the years at Mere. Laura Liebe was born in 1828, and Julia Eliza in 1833; both lived to the end of the first World War in 1918. A third child, Julius, however, was born in 1834 but died in 1837. He is not referred to in Barnes's journal nor is there any mention of him in Lucy Baxter's memoir of her father published in 1887. Julia's health was always a matter of concern to Barnes and this is not to be wondered at considering the physical strain she must have been under. On a number of occasions his diary records 'Giulia malata' and there is even some evidence that she had a still-born child while at Mere. When he left for Dorchester, in 1835, she was the mother of three children under six years. C.J. Wallis, a pupil of Barnes, remembers her as a woman of considerable beauty and also of common-sense. She was a boon to the rather dreamy schoolmaster she had married and he had the sense to know it. Without her, his schools would not have prospered; after her death, they ceased to do so.

The early years of marriage marked for Barnes, as for many other men, an increased flow of energy and an extending range of interests. He read widely, especially in modern languages; he practised regularly with the violin and flute and made up a quartet in May 1832 when Edward Fuller came to stay. There were other concerts at Chantry House with the local curate, Mr R. Cozens and a certain Mr Michell joining the ensemble. Barnes added the pianoforte to his instruments and also regularly played the organ in St Michael's. He even attempted composition and wrote a waltz entitled 'There's a Charm in the Bloom of Youth'. Nor did he neglect the visual arts for, in 1829, he cut wood blocks for John Rutter's *Delineations of Somerset* and also for the Rev Cassan's *Lives of the Bishops of Bath and Wells*. He made engravings on copper for the local silver-smith, Belloni, and spent his earnings on 'plate and trinkets' for Julia. Once she was surprised to find a silver butter-knife with her name engraved on the handle and, on another occasion, to her delight, a pair of silver sugar tongs appeared in the bowl.

Barnes was a practical as well as an academic and artistic man. Much of his spare time was spent in handicrafts, making things for the house and garden. He made arbours and carved chairs, fashioned dolls' cradles and carriages for the children, dug his own garden, painted his own doors, made a box for his engraving tools, carved his own chessboard and chessmen[10] and turned chairlegs upon a lathe in the coach-house. The eccentricity of attire, which became such a delightful quality to his friends in later life, made its first appearance on Mayday 1830, when he tried out a pair of swimming shoes which, according to Lucy Baxter, were flat, like snow shoes, and fitted with valves. The straps broke when he tried them out on the lake but, Lucy claims, he was the successful inventor of a quadrant and an instrument to describe ellipses.

C.J. Wallis has left a description of Barnes in his Mere days. He was a vigorous-looking man of medium height who, after marriage, became a little stout. He was bald from early manhood and his children, when little, thought that a picture of the bald-headed Shakespeare in a book was a portrait of their own papa. Wallis could not help contrasting the entrance into church of the Rector, Henry Wake, and Barnes, the former with his 'quick, sharp step', his look of 'supercilious contempt' and his evident desire to get the service over, and the latter with his 'head and body bent as if to avoid notice' and a manner of meekness and spirituality. Barnes was such a retiring young man that he hated to go out at all. When he did so, he donned a black coat; but he was happier in schoolroom, parlour or garden in his old blue dressing gown, the long skirts of which were always in imminent danger of being chopped off when Barnes was scything his lawn.

For company the Barneses were happy with their infrequent music and supper parties with their few good friends such as Cozens, Card and Mr and Mrs Frederick Smith, teachers of music and dancing, who had recently come to Mere. The schoolmaster's

social position was a doubtful one for he would not be visited by
the rector and the local doctors, lawyers and well-to-do farmers,
yet he was by no means suited to the company of tradesmen
(save the unusually genteel example of Card). C.J. Wallis noticed
that Barnes was always 'pleased to converse with the village-folk
– the rustic ploughman or reaper – but with the trading classes he
was evidently incapable of placing himself on a level of familiarity'. Wallis was puzzled that, while he was a pupil at the
Chantry, 'the physician, the lawyer, the banker and the clergyman . . . looked askance as they passed . . .' But these were days
of social turmoil in the countryside and the schoolmaster and his
wife were bound to provoke suspicion and some contempt
among their affluent neighbours by their mixture of genteel
poverty and threadbare scholarship.[11]

In one pursuit, however, Barnes was very sociable. He loved
the theatre. Once, when comedians visited Mere, he went to the
play every night for a week and was even stimulated to write a
farce himself. In three days in March 1832, he dashed off *The
Blasting of Revenge* and a epilogue entitled *The Honest Thief*. The
players took the manuscript on with them to Wincanton, where
they performed the plays, but no more was heard of the manu-
scripts and the pieces have not survived. Barnes had been all for
throwing everything up to be a playwright and was very disappointed, but his career as a dramatist soon took a different
direction when he became the author of dramatic dialogues set
in the Dorset dialect.

The daily round of school and home was broken perodically by
holidays with Julia's parents at Nailsea or elsewhere. The
summer holiday of 1831 was peculiarly memorable because the
Barneses and Mileses joined forces for an expedition into Wales
as far as Abergavenny. They departed in June and Barnes soon
found himself 'quickened with a yearning to know the Welsh
people and the Welsh speech'. He climbed Borenge, visited
Abergavenny Fair, talked Italian with an exile from his home
land, went fishing in the Usk, walked twenty miles and back to
Llangelly and Nant-y-glo, and even attempted to correct the
Welsh of a native speaker. The visit stimulated in him an interest
in philological studies and he felt that, in Welsh, he had at last
formed an impression of what a 'pure' language was. For the first

time he began to consider why 'educated English' so depended upon Latinate words while the language of village folk in his native Dorset was considered to be the product of ignorance.

There were other holidays with the Mileses, at Nailsea and in the Somerset countryside. Barnes would often take his sketch-book with him and, from the resultant drawings, he produced engravings for his articles in *The Gentleman's Magazine,* and also for Clark's *Avalonian Guide* and Phelps' *History of Somerset.* Unfortunately these holidays came to an abrupt end with the sudden death of James Miles. Barnes recorded in his notebook that his father-in-law was killed 'from a hurt to his spine of the back from the sudden upsetting of his gig, by a heap of soil cast out in the street, and left through a dark evening without any light or warning.' It is interesting that, though she had many sons to choose from, Isabella Miles preferred to go to live with her daughter and son-in-law at Mere. From the 1830s until her death in 1853, she was an invaluable help in the management and domestic affairs of the various Barnes schools and households. She died in February 1853, having outlived her daughter by eight months; she was then eighty-one years old.

Though he now lived in Wiltshire, Barnes continued to take *The Dorset County Chronicle* in order to keep up with affairs in Dorchester and at home in Blackmore. In 1827 he initiated a lifetime of contribution to the paper when he wrote three articles entitled 'Linguiana', which appeared in December. His concern was to explain to *Chronicle* readers that history might be derived from etymology, and his example was taken from the Romans teaching butter and cheese-making to the Saxons. This fact he deduced from the observation that the English, Italian, French and German words for butter are all derived from the Latin 'butyrum'. He corroborates his conclusion from the historical writings of Virgil and Caesar. Elsewhere he traced the histories of such words as 'buttons', 'bellows' and 'chimney' in a manner we might expect from one accustomed to teach foreign languages in the schoolroom.

These early articles were printed above the initials 'W.B.' but Barnes's later pieces in the *Chronicle* were usually signed 'Dilettante', a curiously unsuitable name for one who was noted for his industry and later came to deplore the French element in the

English language. Among the 'Dilettante' contributions is an article entitled 'Pews', which appeared in April 1830, in which he argued that people had been softened by the introductions of such comforts as sofas and carpets, so that they could no longer withstand the blasts of winter. He suggested that more well-to-do parishioners were less attentive in church because they were able to lean back and snooze in pews, while the 'poorer classes' still had to sit up on benches and, consequently, were more attentive. In an article on felons he argued that the criminal transported to Australia was in a better situation than the honest labourer left at home in Dorset, who had to struggle 'against misery on the scanty earning of 1s, or in some cases 6d a day' so that he could buy 'but little firing and less meat' for his family.

The County Chronicle then reserved the top left-hand corner on page two for items headed 'Original Poetry'. Items from nationally-known poets, such as Lord Byron, Mrs Hemans and Mrs Norton, were often printed, but there were also contributions from lesser-known and probably local poets. Most prolific of these was one who signed himself 'M', and whose contributions were usually in the form of sonnets, couched in somewhat vapid terms, and devoted to such popular poetic themes as death, parting, and the yearning of souls. Barnes contributed a 'Sonetto', in Italian, which appeared in August, 1830, and was dedicated to 'M'. He coyly followed this up with a translation which failed to acknowledge that he was translating himself:

> To me no song so sweet no lay so soft,
> As the sweet song of her who sings in grief;
> Of those that sound the lyre of poetry, is none
> Whose strains can penetrate the heart like thine.
> Laura inspired the melancholy troubadour
> Petrarca, but thee the Muse herself inspires,
> Love sweet, though unrequited, swell'd his lyre;
> The graces guide thy hand, sustain thy song,
> Cease not, I pray thee then, sing on for ever;
> Environ'd listen to thy dulcet lays
> Which blunt the edge of keenest suffering;
> O sing again that strain so sad and sweet,
> But may the tears with which thou weepest now
> Be banish'd from thy heart for evermore.'

No doubt the writing of the original was little more than an exercise for him, but it is significant that this diffident young man should choose to come first before the *Chronicle* public in a language not his own.

Barnes was a pioneer in the writing of school textbooks. He was in the practice of 'working up' a set of lesson notes for his teaching purposes and then rewriting them as a primer for use in his own classroom. There was hardly any subject in the school curriculum on which he did not write a primer and, indeed, he was probably the first to write texts on civics and Anglo-Saxon designed for the school classroom. From 1829 to 1835 he wrote four such primers. In the *Etymological Glossary* (1829) he requires his readers to memorise 31 Latin and 15 Greek prefixes, so that they might extend their English vocabularies. When they have mastered the list they are ready to comprehend the examples:

Locus (Lat)	a	place
Col-locate,	v	to place together
Dislocate,	v	to displace
Local,	a	belonging to a place
Locality,	s	the being at a place
Locomotive,	a	a changing place
Locomotion,	s	a changing place

By such ingenious means, the young schoolmaster of Mere was able to help his pupils to relate the language of the ancients to the new world of steam technology. *A Catechism of Government in General and that of England in Particular* appeared in 1833 and proceeded to cross-question the pupil on matters of the constitution: 'Q What is meant by an elective, and what by a hereditary government?' 'A. An elective government is one in which the people choose the successor to a ruler when he dies; and the hereditary one is that in which a ruler is succeeded by his heir or next of kin.' In 1834 appeared *A Few Words on the Advantages of a more common adoption of the Mathematics* in which Barnes argues the unorthodox view that the study is a useful one for gentlemen, on the ground that they will better be able, by pursuing it, to conceive of the world as 'a series of geometrical propositions'. He demonstrated the usefulness of such studies more practically in *A Mathematical Investigation of the Principle of Hanging Doors, Gates, Swing Bridges...'* which was published in 1835 complete with wood engravings by the author. Barnes had only to teach a subject to be excited by it and to want to write a book about it. These little pamphlets are models of lucidity, and their number and range suggest that the author was extending his own education whilst educating others.

While at Mere, Barnes contributed twenty-five papers to the *Gentleman's Magazine*, the earlier ones signed 'Dilettante' and the later ones 'W. Barnes'. The editor of this monthly journal, who was always addressed as 'Mr Urban', soon came to take for granted the extraordinary contributions to scholarship that he received in letters from Mere. Readers would have been amazed to learn that 'Dilettante', who informed them on such matters as the pronunciation of Latin; the habits of the Celts in Spain; Egyptian hieroglyphics and the architecture and monuments of Wessex, was himself a man with no degree and very little schooling. 'Dilettante' wrote on philology, etymology, anthropology, history and literature; he would quote, with obvious understanding, authors in Latin, Hebrew, French, Spanish, Greek and Russian; many of his articles were illustrated with his own engravings. No wonder that Mr Urban was willing to print him so readily!

The first of these articles, which appeared in June 1830, was entitled 'Corruptions of the English Language' and announced, very early in Barnes's life as a philologist, the themes which informed all his later writings on language. As a schoolmaster, and later as a preacher, he was forced to battle with the incomprehension of simple country people who knew nothing of the classical languages. In the *Etymological Glossary*, he had tried to systematise ways of learning foreign words. Now be began to question the wisdom of using these 'borrowed terms' at all:

Since the use of language is to communicate our thoughts to each other, I think that the language which is the most perspicuous (the most easily understood), and the most simple (the most easily learnt), is the best. But if we use ten thousand borrowed words, of which an Englishman has to learn the meaning and sound, instead of as many English ones, of which he knows the meaning and sound without seeking them, we make our language less perspicuous and simple, and consequently less excellent. It may be said that the borrowed words are understood by well-educated people, which I will allow to some extent; but they are critically understood by those only who know the languages from which they are borrowed; and it is no commendation to the English tongue, to say that one must learn three or four others to understand it.'

He developed his argument by pointing out that a 'pure' language was possible – Welsh was a living example – but that English had been 'corrupted' by Gallicising, Latinising and Hellenising tendencies. Thus English was 'fit only for learned people to converse with each other in' while only half a congregation can understand a sermon and only a quarter of children in school understand what they are required to read.

The rest of the article, and its successor in the November issue, tried to persuade its readers to eschew foreign terms wherever possible in favour of English ones. Schoolmasters should encourage the preference of 'ward' to 'protege', of 'wrapper' to 'envelope', of 'end' to 'termination'. Even as early as 1830 he had begun to recommend terms that sound suspiciously like dialect words or neologisms derived from them; rather than 'bigamist', he suggested 'manywedder' and argued that a 'biography' might henceforth be known as a 'lifewrit'. Thus his linguistic sympathies became engaged to notions of a 'pure' English, plainly Saxon in vocabulary, and he found it near at hand in the dialect spoken by his relatives in the Blackmore Vale.

The reader of the *Gentleman's Magazine* who chose to cross pens with Barnes needed to be sure of his ground. A certain Mr A. had argued that the Greek language had been invented by one man. Barnes replied:

My arguments, which A. calls *pseudo-logic,* and which he writes as direct quotation after having put them into *correct logical form,* were directed (as would be seen by referring to them) against the position that the Greek language was invented by *one man,* whom A called 'the inventor of the Greek language'. I used the singular pronoun (he) throughout; and yet A. says, after going through these arguments, 'the inference would be, either that the Greek language would not have been invented, or, if invented, would not have been adopted'. No such thing; the inference would be either that the Greek language would not have been invented by *one man,* or, if invented by *one man* would not have been adopted by others; and, consequently, that it *was not* invented by *one man,* 'the inventor of the Greek language' alluded to by A. The *reductio ad absurdum*, adopted by A. therefore, has not affected my arguments at all.[12]

The thought that this latter-day Locke was confined to a bleak Wiltshire town became a growing annoyance to Julia. She urged him increasingly not to confine his talents to such a 'poor out of the way place' but to seek a larger stage and a better business opportunity for his school. It was agreed between them, in 1835, that they should return once more to Dorchester.

On 26 June, Barnes cast one last wistful look at the lawn he had loved to scythe, and then departed with his young family, his wife and mother-in-law, for his own county again. In Mere he had made a school, taken a wife, become a father and taught himself a number of languages. He had also written some dialect poems which had caused a small stir. These were the Dorset eclogues.

4
The Dorset Eclogues
1834-1835

In 1835, when he left Mere, Barnes had been away from the Blackmore Vale for seventeen years. He had little family left there. His brother, Henry, had died young; James had gone to sea; John and Charles had married away from the Bagber area. Then, in 1826, his only sister, Ann, who had become Mrs Stanley, died in childbirth. John Barnes, his father was still alive but was no great correspondent and what letters he did write amounted to little more than enquiries after his son's health. For news of the Vale, Barnes had to rely upon the gossip relayed from carrier's carts, *The Dorset County Chronicle* and the occasional visit, one of which he made in the spring of 1833 to sketch and take notes for his article on 'the Church at Sturminster Newton', which appeared in the June number of the *Gentleman's Magazine*.

While at Sturminster he stayed with his old friend the Reverend Henry Lane Fox. Why he did not stay with his father is a puzzle. Perhaps the widower felt that he could not entertain, or perhaps the growing social gap between Barnes and his old family friends was a potential embarrassment that both father and son wished to avoid. Whatever the truth of this, Barnes was surprised and disappointed to find that he was barely recognised in Bagber. On reflection he realised that the genteel schoolmaster of a portly and balding appearance was a very different figure from the gregarious laughing boy who had left the town all those years before.

The Vale had changed as well. He remembered it in days of comparative prosperity at the end of the Napoleonic wars. Throughout his young manhood it had still been 'home' to him, a place of childhood joys in which he had been able to count upon the security afforded by an unchanging way of life and a settled community. Now all had changed. The hills at the rim of the Vale had proved no bastion against the troubles that beset rural England. While Barnes had been struggling to establish his school at Mere, the news from Sturminster had been grim. In 1830 the Vale had become the heart of an uprising of agricultural labourers, an event which could have been promoted only by profound suffering on their part.

The economic effect of the wars had been to protect British agriculture against the exports of continental ports. The effects of the blockade were compounded by a series of bad harvests so that, by 1812, the price of wheat had reached the record price of 155 shillings per quarter.[1] The ending of the wars began swiftly to take effect, however, and by December 1813 the price had more than halved and the superabundant harvests of 1814 and 1815 saw it fall further. Farmers were obliged to pay their labourers less and in counties of traditionally low pay, such as Dorset and Wiltshire, wages were often below subsistence level. At the end of the war in 1815, 15% of the population of Dorset was on parish relief.[2] Under the Speenhamland system, farmers often found it more advantageous to contribute to the poor rates than to pay their workers a living wage. The farm workers had never participated in the profits from the boom times and their case now was often desperate. For many their sole diet was one of potatoes and weak tea or 'infusions' of bread scraps and boiling water. They had only the past to look to when:

'Our venerable fathers remember the year
When a man earned three shillings a day and his beer.'

What changed the mood of these workers were stories of a mysterious 'Captain Swing' who was said to ride through the villages of Hampshire, Wiltshire and Dorset, urging the labourers to acts of rick-burning and machine-smashing in attempts to force the farmers to put up wages. In the autumn of 1830 the 'Swing' riots blazed out in the southern counties. The new threshing machines were specially hated objects for the gangs of workers now marching from farm to farm. Many an old score was settled in scenes where money was demanded with scarcely-veiled menace from farmers who may not always have kept their words to their employees in the past. Against all probability, Blackmore was the home of 'the most determined of the Dorset rioters who rose in 1830' and the insurgent labourers were not put down effectively until their resistance was broken by the militia at Castle Hill on 4 December 1830.

The plight of the Dorset labourers had been further exacerbated by the enclosure of much of the common land in the county. Between 1770 and 1830 some six million acres of common land were enclosed in England. The process was often a slow one, applications had to be made, notice of enclosures announced and deeds of agreement signed. Commoners whose families had enjoyed their rights for generations suddenly found that they had been deprived of them. Their livestock was driven from the common and the fences and hedges then went up. More often as not, the news of enclosure had come to the labourers too late for any effectual opposition.[3]

The loss to the commoners was both economic and social. Each villager with commoner rights was entitled to a strip of land to cultivate his vegetables on and also to the benefits of the open common. Here he could graze his cows and his hogs, his goats and his poultry. He was permitted to gather brushwood and furze, as well as mushrooms and berries, fruit and flowers. The open common land was the source of many simples from which homely remedies were concocted. For entire families the common served as the place for exercise and recreation, communal labour and friendly intercourse. Each new generation of village children would first meet when sent out by its parents to roam the common for hazel nuts or blackberries. While the labourer was possessed of common rights he was never merely an employee, one who was wholly dependent upon an employer. Rights in common gave him some status in the village and a say in village affairs. When these rights were stripped away by the innumerable acts of enclosure, the workpeople of English villages found that their voice in community matters was effectively reduced and, even more seriously, that their families were now become entirely dependent upon the goodwill of local farmers for their income.

Throughout his years in Mere, Barnes followed events at home in the Vale very carefully. He heard that, on one Sunday evening in 1830, the congregation of St Mary's Church Sturminster had been read the notice of an act of enclosure of Bagber Common before John Inkpen, the church warden, who formally witnessed the event. During the 1830s and 40s the process of enclosure continued and culminated in 1844 when John Raymond of Shaftesbury acted as the sole commissioner for the 'Agreement for the Inclosure of Bagber Common', by which a number of local farmers took possession of the remainder of the land. Many of these signed the agreement with a simple cross – presumably they could not write – but the principal beneficiary, Lord Rivers, sent his agent, Robert Harvey, to sign for him.[4] The agreement was designed to 'inclose such open and Common piece of land and to extinguish the right of commonage' which had belonged to the humble families of Bagber, the Barnes, the Rabbetts and others, for hundreds of years.

The depression in agriculture and the effects of enclosure were felt in Mere as well as in Bagber. The Swing riots were even more widespread in Wiltshire than in Dorset. The young schoolmaster must have heard much talk in the market or among the knots of men gathered outside the Ship and the Talbot inns as they discussed the plight of their industry and the fears of insurrection in the countryside.

The problems of the farmers affected his school as well as other local industries, and added to his difficulties when he tried to recruit more scholars or to extract overdue fees. His letters to *The Dorset County Chronicle* had made plain his own instinctive sympathy with the labouring people but he had to be careful in expressing such feelings for fear that his sentiments would sound very like radicalism and encouragement to insurrection. Such impressions on behalf of the parents would have ended his school overnight.

Yet his heart went out to the labourers and the tenant farmers enduring such misfortune. His own uncle and aunt, Charles and Ann Rabbetts, had personified for him the useful, hard-working and kindly sort of tenant farmers who had provided work for others and treated their workpeople well. Uncle had once been able to boast that he was 'out o' debt an' out o' danger'[5], but he too had become a victim of the fall in prices; Barnes had attended the selling up of Pentridge Farm, after which Aunt Ann had died of a broken heart:

Alas a sale is generally followed by a change of circumstances and that is a thing which, at best, fills the mind with solicitude; but the feelings of an honest man in the last case are horrible. The thought of coming poverty makes him sad, the necessary dispersion of his children chills his heart; he trembles with agony when he thinks of the sorrows and sufferings of his wife, and the villainy of men who have cheated and deserted him, almost excites him to madness; but he reflects on the former goodness of God and remembers his sins and weeps. A sale of the last mentioned kind of an uncle's stock, and which I saw when a boy, made on my mind a strong impression. My uncle was a farmer in the West of England, but became insolvent from the depression of the agricultural interest after the end of the French war. My aunt had a numerous family, and her long exercised solicitude as a mother, and her continual struggles against misfortune had nearly brought her with sorrow to the grave; she was calm, and it was only when one of her daughters passed her, that a tear rolled down her sallow cheek.

The young men were in that severe and reckless mood in which men are usually thrown when assailed by misfortune which they can still resist.

The girls were bewildered, and scarcely knew what happened around them; then were driven away the cows under which the weeping milk-maid had so often sung the simple songs of the country; then went the wagon in which the merry haymakers had so many times ridden to the feast of harvest-home; and in short, then everything that was dear from familiarity was taken away, and my uncle as he looked on the fields he had so long cultivated with hope, and of which he had taken the produce in grateful joy, sighed and dropped a tear as if he had said, "DULCIA LINQUIMUS ARVA."[6]

Such memories of the people of the Vale moved Barnes deeply but he dared not express his sympathies too openly for fear that he might be misinterpreted by the farmers and tradesmen he was canvassing for pupils. What he wished to do was to persuade the more fortunate members of the community to enter imaginatively into the plight of the poor. He needed to write not statements of opinion but vivid accounts of the lives of people of the Vale so that others might regard them with respect and sympathy. If he could employ humour to this end, so much the better.

On 2 February 1834 the readers of that most conservative of journals, *The Dorset County Chronicle*, opened their copies to find a verse curiosity, a poem with a Latin title but written in the dialect of local workpeople. It was *Rusticus Dolens Or Inclosures of Common*. Barnes subsequently noted in his scrapbook: 'I wrote the first of my Poems of Rural Life in the Dorset Dialect others were written from time to time for many years. They were printed in *The Dorset County Chronicle* – The first Dorset Idyl was written in my room when I was uphalening from a sickness an ailing liver.'[7] The piece was described to the readers as an 'Eclogue' and, though its mode was an antique one, its theme was contemporary. In the poem, two labouring men, Thomas and Richard, discuss the effects of the new enclosures. John explains that he is taking his geese to market because 'they do mean to take the moor in' i.e. to enclose it. He explains to his friend that he will also have to get rid of his cow because he will no longer have anywhere to graze her. The two men reflect on the usefulness of a common to people of their background:

JOHN

Aye, that's the thing, you zee. Now I do mow
My bit o' grass, an' meäke a little rick;
An' in the zummer, while do grow,
My cow do run in common vor to pick
A bleäde or two o' grass, if she can vind em,
Vor tother cattle don't leäve much behind em.
Zoo in the evenen, we do put a lock
O' nice fresh grass avore the wicket;
An' she do come at vive or zix o'clock,
As constant as the zun, to pick it.
An' then, bezides the cow, why we do let
Our geese run out among the emmet hills;
An' then when we do pluck em, we do get
Vor zeäle zome veathers an' zome quills;
An' in the winter we do fat em well,
An' car em to the market vor to zell
To gentlevo'ks, vor we don't oft avvword
To put a goose a-top ov ouer bwoard;
But we do get our feäst, – vor we be eäble
To clap the giblets up a-top o'teäble.

THOMAS

An' I don't know o' many better things,
Than geese's heads and gizzards, lags an' wings.

JOHN

An' then, when I ha' nothen else to do,
Why I can teäke my hook an' gloves, an' goo
To cut a lot o' vuzz and briars
Vor heten ovens, or vor lighten viers.
An' when the children be too young to eärn
A penny, they can g'out in zunny weather,
An' run about, an' get together
A bag o' cow-dung vor to burn.

THOMAS

'Tis handy to live near a common;
But I've a-zeed, an' I've a-zaid,
That if a poor man got a bit o'bread,
They'll try to teäke it vrom en.
But I wer twold back tother day,
That they be got into a way
O' letten bits o' groun' out to the poor.[8]

In the following issue, readers were again provided with a
dialect poem. *Rusticus Gaudens or The Allotment System* takes up a
point from the previous eclogue, the value of allotments which
may in part recompense the poor man for his rights in common.
Unfortunately not all landowners were prepared to offer their
workers the chance of allotments. Barnes is clearly in favour of
the idea and his protagonist in the poem, Richard, explains the
advantages of allotments to the less fortunate John:

RICHARD

O, 'tis a goodish help to woone, I'm sure o't.
If I had not a-got it, my poor bwones
Would now ha' eäch'd a-cracken stwones
Upon the road; I wish I had zome mwore o't.

JOHN

I wish the girt woones had a-got the greäce
To let out land lik' this in ouer pleäce;
But I do fear there'll never be nwone vor us,
An' I can't tell whatever we shall do:
We be a most a-starven, an' we'd goo
To 'merica, if we'd enough to car us.

RICHARD

Why 'twer the squire, good now! a worthy man,
That vu'st brought into ouer pleäce the plan;
He zaid he'd let a vew odd eäcres
O' land to us poor leab'ren men;
An', faïth, he had enough o' teäkers
Vor that, an' twice so much ageän.
Zoo I took zome here, near my hovel,
To exercise my speäde an' shovel;
An' what wi' dungen, diggen up, an' zeeden,
A-thinnen, cleänen, howen up an' weeden,
I, an' the biggest o' the children too,
Do always vind some useful jobs to do. [9]

The poem ends with a marvellously detailed explanation of all
the benefits gained by keeping a pig. The animal, we are informed, can be fed upon the 'little taties' which are too small for
human consumption. It will provide handsome flitches either for
sale or the chimney corner, and will supply offal, 'netlins for to
boil' and blood for black puddings.

What were the readers of *The Dorset County Chronicle* to make
of such stuff? The editors were fairly clear about the material for
they published six such eclogues in just over a year. This writing
was worthy of publication because it employed a dialect form
which would amuse their local readership. But it was not poetry.
True poetry always appeared in 'poet's corner', that is at the top
left hand corner of page two under the heading 'Original Poetry'.
A number of Barnes's sonnets had appeared in this prestigious
position but the eclogues appeared low down on pages two or
three among the farm reports and stock news. When Barnes
wrote a poem beginning: 'When in the happy dreams of silent
night/ My soul roams back to some sweet youthful scene' he was
considered to be writing true poetry, an art which concerned
itself with roaming souls rather than the constituents of black
puddings. Most readers probably concurred. For many of them
the eclogues were jokes. Poems in the local dialect were inevitably humorous because the language of the work people was
both a matter for amusement in itself and an hilarious absurdity
when arranged rhythmically so as to resemble 'true' poetry, its
linguistic antithesis. To decorate the resultant confection with

a pompous Latin title was to colour the joke further. The first review that ever appeared of Barnes's dialect poetry came out in the *Chronicle* on 16 January 1834:

To the Editor of the Dorset County Chronicle and Somersetshire Gazette.

Sir—The Dialogue headed 'Rusticus Dolens' in your paper of the 2nd instant is inimitable and doubtless caused great merriment to those who really understand the Dorset dialect. Now, Sir, from 27 years constant residence in a country village of your county, I consider myself a tolerably good judge of the lingo. I would therefore in kindness point out two errors, which might be avoided in any future effusion the writer may favor us with. In the first line 'morn' should be written 'murn', and the word 'vor', which occurs very often, should be written 'var'. These alterations may appear trifling; but, Sir, I am a stickler for the purity of our native dialect, which must plead the apology of
Your obedient Servant,

CRITIC
Jan 11, 1834

Barnes subsequently discovered 'Critic' to be the Rev Frederick Urquhart, the Rector of Broadmayne. Urquhart probably spoke for most readers in that his attention to the first of the eclogues ignored the matter for the manner. The 'inimitability' of the poems lay in their employment of the dialect as a mode of expression. It is difficult to conclude anything other than that his response is a facetious one and that to be a 'stickler for purity' in what is a mere 'lingo' is Urquhart's notion of a joke. The eclogues were written in dialect and *therefore* they must be considered to be comic. Quite clearly, Wordsworth's stricture that poetry should be 'the real language of men' had not influenced the poetic conventions in counties such as Dorset. The verses appearing in poet's corner employed a stock diction to convey sentiments as lofty as they were vapid. Souls and dreams and partings were the proper stuff of poetry, not geese's gizzards, the price of bread and children gathering cow dung. As for the rural muse, the *Chronicle* gave full attention to such poems as *My Native Village and other Poems*, by N.T. Carrington, replete with such sentiments as:

'Bard of the village! o'er thy peaceful grave
The bay should brighten, and the laurel wave:-
Thy lyre no more shall charm the sylvan bower,
Or soothe the hearth in winter's dreary hour.

'Carrington's muse' concluded the *Chronicle*, 'is accompanied in all her excursions by Nature as her lovely handmaid. The Graces are still in her train, the Seasons scatter her path with roses, and all Creation opens its inexhaustible stores to view.'[10]

It is of the nature of genius not that it invents entirely new elements in human life but that it combines familiar elements in uniquely fresh ways. Barnes drew upon his whole life in writing the eclogues and it may well be that, at first, even he did not recognise the significance of his achievement and its potentiality for poetic development. His translations of Petrarch drew only from his reading, but his eclogues drew upon both literature and life. In this respect he may be likened to other major poets of the century, Hopkins and Kipling for example, whose achievement consists chiefly in resisting prevailing literary influences in order to invent or rediscover unique forms of poetic utterance.

We may distinguish five elements of Barnes's experience which are unified in the eclogues. The chief impulse behind them lies in the deep affection with which he regards Dorset labouring people and his knowledge of their way of life. These poems, and their successors, owe their objective sharpness to the detailed recollections he possessed of his friends and neighbours in Blackmore days. No less important is the wonderfully attentive ear he brought to Blackmore speech so that it is in the eclogues that we hear for the first time the authentic cadences of the dialect of the county. Thirdly, Barnes was a keen reader of newspapers and a shrewd observer of national affairs. In the six dialogues written in 1834/5 he succeeded in relating large national events to the felt experience of humble labouring men and women. His reflections on life were always informed by his readings of literature. Many of his best poems were dramatic pieces and, though his farces were failures in the theatre at Wincanton, his dramatic dialogues were the subject of delighted comment all over the county. Finally, it was from his readings in the classics, and from Virgil in particular, that he found his models for the Dorset eclogues.

Barnes's feat of transposing the themes of Virgil's ten eclogues into local and contemporary expression was a considerable achievement. In retrospect, the potentiality of Latin eclogues as models for Dorset dialogues may seem an obvious insight but such a judgement is a measure of Barnes's originality in seeing a likeness where nobody else did. Furthermore, the relationship was between two polar opposites, for, as we have seen, the eclogues were thought of as part of high culture and learning, whereas the speech of country people was often a matter of ridicule to their betters. But in the long evenings spent poring over Virgil, while his pupils larked in the little playground by the church at Mere, Barnes was musing on poems from the ancient world which strangely blended in his mind with the news from the Blackmore Vale. In Virgil's first eclogue Meliboeus grieves over his necessary exile from familiar fields, just as the emigrant Dorset labourers must have regretted their loss of the sights of home. In the third eclogue Barnes discovered a rural singing match which he retold as the boasting rivalry of two Dorset labourers in his poem *The Best Man in the Field*. Elsewhere in Virgil he found themes of dispossession and exile, as well as the countryman's delight in his flocks. In the eighth eclogue he found a refrain which ran 'Make Daphnis come home now, come home now, my spells!' which he refashioned into a Dorset dialogue entitled *Father Come Home*.[11]

In an article in *The Gentleman's Magazine* in 1832, Barnes observed of Virgil's poems that they 'were for example, in praise of female charms and of excellent persons on love and they were sometimes of a comic kind.'[12] The third of his own eclogues, which appeared on 3 April 1834, was of the comic kind. It was *Rusticus Narrans, A Cousin down from London*, written first as a dialogue but later, more effectively, as a monologue. The theme is the old one of town versus country and involves the bucolic revenge of the speakers upon an urban relative who thinks himself smart. In the earlier version Cousin Sam is made to pay for his swaggering and patronising attitudes by being tossed by Sorrel the horse, butted into a dungheap by a lamb and chased by a bull. The chief narrator, Stephen, concludes that:

'They cockneys that do think therzelves so cunnen
Be noggerheads when they be out o' Lon'on.'[13]

Barnes appended a few short notes to this eclogue for the benefit of the readers of the *Chronicle*. He points out that a 'jack o' lint' is the common name for a scarecrow or ragman in some parts of Dorset. It is interesting that, even in his own county news-paper in an early decade of the nineteenth century, he felt com-pelled to explain some of the dialect terms of the poetry. In doing so he attempted to forestall the objection that he was to receive for the rest of his life, that poetry written in Dorset dialect was unintelligible to the 'polite' reader. Barnes also attempted to distance himself from the sentiments expressed in *A Cousin down from London* by adding the note: 'The polite townsman must not consider these sentiments as the Author's own.' In his position as a private schoolmaster in a country town, he could afford to offend no one.

In the spring and summer of 1834, the prevailing talk in Dor-chester was of the trial of six labourers from the village of Tol-puddle who, on 19 March at the Old Crown Court, had been sentenced to seven year's transportation to the Australian colo-nies for illegally taking an oath in the formation of a friendly society for agricultural labourers. For weeks the *Chronicle* had been anticipating trouble among the farm workers whose pay had recently dipped below subsistence level on many farms. The sentence upon the Tolpuddle 'Martyrs' was excessively severe and almost certainly influenced by the magistrates' memories of the recent 'Swing' riots. On 24 March some ten thousand people met in London to protest at the punishment and, in April, Robert Owen addressed another meeting of thirty thousand in Copen-hagen Fields.[14] So powerful was the agitation that followed that, after much procrastination, the Home Secretary, Lord John Russell, agreed to a full and free pardon for all the men on 14 March 1836.

It is sometimes stated that Barnes offered no response to these great national events centred upon his own town. E.M. Forster noted of him that: 'He could live through the shadows of the Labourer's Revolt in 1830 without its shadows falling across his verse.' Trevor Hearl has suggested that Barnes would have been greatly embarrassed by an incident in which his own natural sympathy for the plight of the working people would have been tempered by his disapproval of the methods of trades unionism.[15]

In 1874 Barnes pasted the obituary of George Loveless, the martyrs' leader, into his scrapbook but added no comment.

Hearl is almost certainly right in his conclusions. We know of Barnes's concern for the farmworkers whose 1s or 6d a day could buy 'but little firing and less meat'. We also know that Barnes disliked organised labour, for he subsequently wrote a poem entitled *The Times*, in which the Chartist is characterised as a cunning crow who persuades the naive labourer, represented as a pig, to grout up a field for him with the promise of roots. As a result, the crow gets the ears of corn turned up by the pig while the latter gets nothing but a beating.[16] Barnes's dislike of the martyrs' action was furthered by his acquaintanceship with a number of the magistrates in the case and also by the Methodism of the accused. Nevertheless, Barnes's disapproval for the manner of the farmworker's actions was at least equalled by his concern for their plight. The trouble was that he was constrained by his professional position from an open expression of sympathy for the farmworkers' situation. Any commentary he was to make had to be an oblique one.

The eclogue *A Cousin down from London*, appeared fifteen days after the sentencing of the labourers but was probably written before that date. Perhaps Barnes was more affected by the sentence than at first appears for no further eclogue was published until seven months later, November. That poem was *Rusticus Emigrans*, the theme of which was the feelings of a labourer forced by poverty to emigrate to Van Dieman's Land, the destination reserved by the magistrates for George Loveless himself. In *Rusticus Emigrans* Barnes is clearly not in the mood for the comic portrayal of the farm worker; the tone is one of sober resignation when Richard explains to Robert that he must go to 'Dieman's Land' because he can no longer support his family at home. When Robert enquires how Richard feels to leave his birthplace and friends behind the reply is a lament whose power is reinforced by its simplicity:

RICHARD

When I do think o' be'en piarted
Vrom al my friends var ever, I could cry
But var the shiame o' be'en so softhearted.

Here be the trees that I did use to climb in,
Here is the brook that I did use to zwim in,
Here be the ground where I've a worked and played;
Here is the hut that I wer barn and bred in;
Here is the little church where we've a prayed,
And churchyard that my kinsvolk's buones be laid in;

And I myzelf, you know, should like to lie
Among 'em too when I do come to die;
But 'tis noo use to have zich foolish wishes;
I shall be tossed, i' may be, to the vishes.[17]

Millions of such labourers as Richard were driven to emigrate with their families in the nineteenth century yet *Rusticus Emigrans* remains one of the few poetic attempts to describe its impact on the immigrant. The effect of Barnes's best eclogues such as this one was not merely to humanise the country labourer but also to dignify him in the eyes of middle-class *Chronicle* readers.

It must be admitted, however, that dignity is not a feature of *Rusticus Rixans*, or *The Best Man in the Field* which appeared on Christmas Day and which probably had its origins in Virgil's third eclogue (a singing contest between shepherds). *Rusticus Rixans* is the poorest of this series of eclogues and amounts to little more than an exchange of bucolic abuse in which the protagonists address each other as 'noggerhead' and 'slobber-chops'. What is of more interest is that Barnes provided a glossary for *Chronicle* readers of the more technical terms used in haymaking. We learn that 'tedding' means to 'throw the grass abroad after it is mowed' and that 'pooks' are cones of drying hay. He also adds a sharply-worded final observation:

There is a false notion among many who do not understand rural matters, that in the field of work of the labourer there is no skill. Let them try to make a rick, build a load of hay, or strike a stroke in mowing; or let them whet a scythe and see how long they will rub before they bring up the test of good whetting, the thread on the edge. A London apprentice should not laugh at a rustic because he cannot dance a quadrille, and knows nothing of the drama; since he of the town knows nothing of crops, cattle, and correctives of soil; and would be as awkward in a field as the other in a ballroom . . .[18]

The Dorset eclogues had begun as a half humorous set of observations of country workpeople but, having invented such poems, they became, for Barnes, the instrument for his passionate championship of their way of life. The final poem of the series was *Rusticus Domi* or *Father Come Home*, which seeks to display the domestic life and humble hopes of a hard-working labourer's family. The poem begins with the wife and child awaiting the father at the end of the day:

CHILD

O mother, mother! be the teäties done?
Here's father now a-comen down the track.
He's got his nitch o'wood upon his back,
An' such a speäker in en! I'll be bound,
He's long enough to reach vrom ground
Up to the top ov ouer tun:
'Tis jist the very thing vor Jack an' I
To goo a-colepecksen wi' by an' by.

WIFE

The teäties must be ready pretty nigh;
Do teäke woone up upon the fork an' try.
The ceäke upon the vier, too, 's a-burnen,
I be afeärd: do run an' zee, an' turn en.[19]

The conversation turns upon the family economy; John reckons that he has three more weeks of hedging to count upon, and perhaps some trenching and felling after that. He hopes to 'rub on pretty well' till summer. In exchanges of gathering optimism father, mother and child proffer their little bits of good news. The little girl announces proudly that she is to go picking stones for Farmer True the following week at threepence a day, and that her small brother is to get twopence for scaring birds. She tries to wheedle her father into making a cracker for her but he is too tired and prefers to sit in front of the fire eating the apple cake his wife has made for him.

No poem provides the rural historian with more detail of the domestic life of the time than does *Father Come Home*. There is a determined cheerfulness about the family which Barnes clearly finds admirable, and he must have believed that he had provided a picture of the rural worker at his best; hardworking, useful, uncomplaining and cheerful. But the poem raises more questions than it settles. Can it be for the best that the income for this little family is so precarious? Have they nothing to look forward to but a life of unrelieved toil? What would happen if the father became ill and could not 'rub along' till summer? Barnes's poetry does not answer such questions; it was left to the novels of Thomas Hardy to do so. What Barnes does offer us is social documentary which is informed by an undoubted sharpness of eye and authenticity of detail. To this he adds a deftness of characterisation, an immediacy of dramatic situation and a vigour of dialect language which enables him to surpass Crabbe and Clare in conveying the thought and feeling of the rural poor. The notes to these poems elicited all the enthusiasm he had previously conferred upon classical language. For him, old words have all the sweetness and savour of cider apples; he loves to produce an antiquated term, to polish it gently and then to provide a learned gloss upon it:

Colepecksen – cullpecksing. Searching for and beating down the few apples that may be left on the trees after the crop is taken in. The young urchins turn over almost every leaf in this apple bunt. The verb, I think, is properly to *cullpecks,* to cull pecks, i.e., to gather small quantities.[20]

In such writing, poetry and philology have come together.

Barnes continued to write eclogues for many years but those published in 1834/5 established the form. Later he wrote of the amalgamation of small tenant farms, of the new poor laws and again of emigration. Perhaps his finest poem on a social theme, however, is not an eclogue but a splendid diatribe against further enclosure entitled *The Leane:*

> They do zay that a travellen chap
>   Have a'put in the newspeäper now,
> That the bit o' green ground on the knap
>   Should be all a-took in vor the plough.
>
> He do fancy 'tis easy to show
>   That we can be but stunpolls at best,
> Vor to leäve a green spot where a flower can grow,
>   Or a voot-weary walker mid rest.
> 'Tis hedge-grubben, Thomas, an' ledge-grubben,

Never a-done
While a sov'ren mwore's to be won.

The road, he do zay, is so wide
    As 'tis wanted vor travellers' wheels,
As if all that did travel did ride
    An' did never get galls on their heels.
He would leäve sich a thin strip o' groun',
    That, if a man's veet in his shoes
Wer a-burnen an' zore, why he coulden zit down
    But the wheels would run over his tooes.
Vor 'tis meäke money, Thomas, an' teäke money,
    What's zwold an' bought
Is all that is worthy o' thought.[21]

Barnes always detested that attitude which turns all life into money-making. It was not commercial enterprise which England lacked in his view, but the wisdom to value what was beyond price. His own philosophy of life was gentle, uncommercial and humanistic.

In inventing the Dorset eclogues Barnes had hit upon the dialect poetry for which he was later to become celebrated. The 'Hwomely Rhymes' of later years contain both lyric and narrative poems but it was the eclogue which came first and enabled Barnes to fuse his dramatic skill with his splendid linguistic recollection. Not all the eclogues of later years deal with social themes. The favourite among the audiences to which he read in later years was *A Bit O' Sly Coortin* in which the lovers, John and Fanny, meet, have a jealous tiff, and then make up again. His Dorset audiences recognised in it the age old story of country lovers carrying out a little courting under the hedge after a hard day's work. Fanny is frightened of the trouble she will get into if her parents see them, but John is aflame with jealousy:

JOHN

I thought you mid be out wi' Jemmy Bleäke.

FANNY

An' why be out wi' him, vor goodness' seäke?

JOHN

You walk'd o' Zunday evenen wi'n, d'ye know, You went vrom church a-hitch'd up in his eärm.

FANNY

Well, if I did, that werden any harm.
Lauk! that is zome'at to teäke notice o'.

JOHN

He took ye roun' the middle at the stile,
An' kiss'd ye twice 'ithin the ha'f a mile.

FANNY

Ees, at the stile, because I shoulden vall,
He took me hold to help me down, that's all;
An' I can't zee what very mighty harm
He could ha' done a-lenden me his eärm.
An' as vor kissen o' me, if he did,
I didden ax en to, nor zay he mid:
An' if he kiss'd me dree times, or a dozen,
What harm wer it? Why idden he my cousin?
An' I can't zee, then, what there is amiss
In cousin Jem's jist gi'en me a kiss.

JOHN

Well, he shan't kiss ye, then; you shan't be kiss'd
By his girt ugly chops, a lanky houn'!
If I do zee'n, I'll jist wring up my vist
An' knock en down.
I'll squot his girt pug-nose, if I don't miss en;
I'll warn I'll spweil his pretty lips vor kissen!

FANNY

Well, John, I'm sure I little thought to vind
That you had ever sich a jealous mind.
What then! I s'pose that I must be a dummy,
An' mussen go about nor wag my tongue
To any soul, if he's a man, an' young;
Or else you'll work yourzelf up mad wi' passion,
An' talk away o' gi'en vo'k a drashen,
An' breaken bwones, an' beäten heads to pummy!
If you've a-got sich jealous ways about ye,
I'm sure I should be better off 'ithout ye.

JOHN

Well, if girt Jemmy have a-won your heart,
We'd better break the coortship off an' peärt.

FANNY

He won my heart! There, John, don't talk sich stuff;
Don't talk noo mwore, vor you've a-mind enough.
If I'd a-lik'd another mwore than you,
I'm sure I shoulden come to meet ye zoo;
Vor I've a-twold to father many a storry,
An' took o' mother many a scwolden vor ye.
                    (weeping)
But 'twull be over now, vor you shan't zee me
Out wi' ye noo mwore, to pick a quarrel wi' me.[22]

This is the world of Shakespearian comedy; we smile at the little vexations of the lovers' lives in the serene knowledge that Jack shall have his Jill again and all will be well. The poem is a triumphant vindication of the view that the Dorset eclogues are equally suited to themes gay as well as grave.

5

A Professional Man, Dorchester
1835-1847

In the evening of 26 June 1835 as the shadow of St Peter's Church tower lengthened down High East Street in Dorchester, it was met by a removal wagon laden with household goods trundling up the hill. The vehicle turned left into Cornmarket and then left again into Wood and Stone Lane, sometimes known as Durngate Street. It stopped on the corner with Church Lane and William Barnes climbed down to survey the building he had chosen to be his first school in Dorchester.[1]

The front door opened and his young family came out to greet him having preceded him from Mere that morning by coach. Julia was carrying their infant son, Julius, while the two little girls, Laura Liebe aged six and Julia Eliza aged two rushed out to tell Papa of their new home. They were quickly hushed by Mrs Miles, his capable mother-in-law, who intructed the tranter and his men as to the positions in the house in which items of furniture were to be placed. As he supervised the unloading Barnes felt a tremor of unease for his little family. Only this morning he had watched the early mist for the last time over the lake in his beloved garden at Chantry House. He had exchanged the cool loveliness of the terraced greensward at Mere, with its waterfall and whispering row of elms, for this mean house on a narrow dusty street. The idyll was over.

Julia was too busy attending to the children to give way to such thoughts. She had concluded correctly that there was a wider prospect for her family in the narrow lanes of Dorchester than in all the space of the old Chantry House. Had not Mr Pople, a native of Dorchester, written to William to inform him that 'Ours is a town in which the inhabitants are well off' and urging him to take a school there? Pople was right. Barnes reported later in his notebook that 'boys came in very hopefully and we soon had a fair and fast-filling school.'² The town was already an educational centre for the county although, it is true, that Durngate Street was at the wrong end of town to attract the better families of potential parents. The more fashionable location for schools such as the Dorchester Grammar School or Hardye's, as it was known, was on the southern, Weymouth side. Yet Durngate Street was a foothold.

The loss of Chantry House at first affected all of them, even Julia. Barnes noted that 'we did not feel the happiness of the change in the strait pent house instead of the old Chantry House with its open garden.' But he soon learned to stifle the ache in his heart by attention to work. He had a school to make and practical tasks to attend to; he had to set up house, canvass parents, buy beds and books and crockery. He had to settle his family and to teach all day without help. Julia and her mother were equally busy making arrangements to welcome twenty boarders and as many day boys, as well as cooking for the Barnes family of three adults and three children.

The return of the family to Dorchester had not been merely a matter of business calculation, for both Barnes and Julia had felt the pull of the old county town in which they had first met and courted years before. Such sentimental memories, complemented by the urgings of Pople and their old friend Frederick Smith, had proved an irresistible argument. In that same year of 1835, Smith himself had removed his highly successful dancing academy from Mere to Dorchester and his continued company was a great attraction to the Barnes family. Nevertheless, Barnes was aware of the presence in Dorchester of a number of rival schools such as 'Mr Watson's School for Young Gentlemen' and Hardye's school kept by the Reverend Richard Cutler. Barnes's fees were initially designed to be very competitive. Cutler charged forty guineas a year for a boarder whereas Barnes's fees were relatively modest. In an advertisement for the school written just prior to its establishment, he announced that 'For all the Common Branches of Boarders under 12 years old' he would charge 22 guineas; for those over twelve 24 guineas and for day boys, 5 guineas. So successful was he that, seven years later in 1844; when he chose to advertise in the *Fashionable Guide to Dorchester and Weymouth*, he felt able to ask fifty pounds a year for 'parlour boarders', thirty pounds for boarders and ten pounds for day boys. The considerable difference might partly be explained by inflation but it was also a measure of Barnes's effectiveness as a schoolmaster.

In his two years at Durngate Street, Barnes gave all his energies to establishing himself as a professional schoolmaster in the eyes of the town. While there and at Norman House, he became something of an educational pioneer. He introduced new methods of tuition; exhaustively researched and expanded the school's curriculum; wrote detailed lesson plans which he eventually published as a series of textbooks covering most of the school syllabus. Above all, he provided an unusually sound and enlightened education for hundreds of boys in an atmosphere which was more of a happy home than the brutalised institution which many contemporary schools had become. He was not only a kindly master but an affectionate one, and he retained the friendship of many of his pupils after their school lives ended.

Despite the intense professional efforts of the early days at Durngate Street, his mind naturally craved other occupations and interests. Opportunities for scything, gardening and wood-turning were not plentiful in a small Dorchester house jam-packed with children nor, regretfully, was there much quiet leisure for engraving. Besides, his interests were now more academic than in his early days at Mere. Instead he turned to study and writing of a private nature. He made friends with a certain Colonel Besant, the author of *The Persian and Urdu Letter-Writer*, who was willing to read these languages with him once a week. In the evenings he was sometimes able to steal a few moments from other activities:

It was my way . . . to pass much of the play time and evening in a study within sight of the playground or within call of the boys or the ushers and so I worked, even against the irksomeness of lonely confinement and I found the thoughts and work of the Dorset idylls to refreshen rather than weary my mind.[3]

Though the idyll was over there was no reason why he should not create others in his imagination. He later found that he needed to defend himself against the charge of negligence for writing poetry while he should have been supervising his pupils, hence his subsequent insistence upon the re-creative nature of poetic composition.

The curriculum at Durngate Street was the extraordinarily wide one that Barnes had pioneered at Chantry House and was still developing. He had advertised his school as one for 'Young Gentlemen intended for Professions connected with Civil or Military Engineering, Mechanics, Surveying, Architecture, or Navigation . . . and those who may need a Classical Education'. With no ushers to help him at the outset he was still able to offer 'Latin, · Greek, French, Italian, German or other European Language' as well as to 'render valuable service to Gentlemen going out to India, by teaching them to read the Asiatic Character, and the Rudiments of that essential and all-sufficient language in Asia, the Persian as well as the Hindoostanee'. In the mornings he continued his series of lectures, mostly on scientific subjects, and, wherever possible, provided demonstrations in 'botany, natural history, physics, chemistry, electricity and geology.'[4] To this end he purchased scientific instruments out of his own pocket, such as the mysterious 'Periphan' ordered from Baker's of Weymouth, in 1845, at a cost of £3.8s.6d with box.

Lucy Baxter has pointed out that her father's object in his early morning scientific lectures was not only to render the subject comprehensible but interesting. One of his pupils, Octavius Pickard Cambridge, remembered that 'Each scholar had to take down a proposition (derived from the lecture) generally embracing one point only . . . Notes were to be taken upon the lecture, which was always illustrated by objects and experiments, and an examination upon it was subsequently made'.[5] This system of teaching science seems to have been generally successful for a number of Barnes's pupils later became eminent scientists. Pickard Cambridge became a world-famous arachnologist, J.B. Lock lectured in mathematics and physics at Gonville & Caius College, Cambridge, and Frederick Treves won a knighthood as sergeant surgeon to Edward VII.

Barnes's teaching of science was remarkably advanced because he encouraged his pupils to observe and experiment as well as to listen. He frequently led excursions into the countryside surrounding Dorchester: 'Sometimes the boys vied with each other who should find the greatest number of 'Cruciferous'

or 'Composite' flowers; other days they went armed with ham-
mer and bags for a geological expedition, finding specimens of
terebratulae, echinus or belemnite in the chalk cutting of the
then new railway.'[6] Once there was an incident which amply
demonstrated Barnes's puckish sense of humour:

'Come down Blair, said the master to the boy on a branch of an elm, 'we
are going on now'.
'I'm coming directly, sir,' cried Blair as well as he could speak, with his
mouth full of linnet's eggs. He had hardly said the words when the
branch cracked, and the boy came suddenly down with a good deal of
clutching at saving branches in his descent.
As soon as William Barnes found that his pupil was not hurt, he remarked dryly, 'You kept your word, Blair; I like a boy who speaks the
truth.'[7]

As the school flourished, so did his family. Lucy Emily, his
third daughter was born in January 1837, and it became apparent
that he needed larger premises for both his home and school. He
found what he needed at Norman's House, next to Napper's
Mite, on the east side of South Street. Here he had the use of a
three-storey building, in a fashionable area for schools, whose
small top-floor study overlooked the yard which acted as a playground for his scholars at the back. He was now able to expand
his school to fifty boys and was soon turning away pupils. Even
in a town as rural as Dorchester, the small tradesmen and professional men who formed the bulk of his parents were beginning
to feel the effects of the national prosperity arising from increased industrialisation. They wanted a sound education for
their sons at reasonable prices and Barnes was able to supply it.
His instruction was sound, his curriculum included mathematics, mechanics and science, his establishment was well-
ordered and pious; his reputation respectable. Why should not
such an effective schoolmaster himself hope to participate in the
general prosperity enjoyed by other professional men?

It soon became plain that Barnes would need extra help, and he
provided it by appointing a long succession of ushers. C.J.
Wallis, an old pupil, was with him until 1839, and Julius Miles,
his own brother-in-law, until 1840. Barnes was unusual among
Victorian schoolmasters in that he took his responsibilities in
teacher-training seriously, and he gave help to both these young

men. After a number of brief appointments, Isaac Hann joined him and remained with him as a senior usher from 1842-1855. Hann was a native of Blackmore Vale and a distant relative of the Hardys of Bockhampton. He was a reliable man but of limited intellectual abilities. Barnes once told Thomas Hardy an anecdote of Hann which shows that the usher had a very quick temper. Apparently, Napoleon III, while exiled in England, was for a time the guest of Colonel Dawson-Damer at Came House. One Sunday afternoon, Damer accompanied his guest in promenading upon the town 'Walks', then a regular part of the local social life. On passing Barnes and Hann, who were also promenading, the future emperor slipped his cane between the legs of the humble usher, causing him to stumble. At once Hann flushed with rage and took off his coat with a challenge to the foreigner to fight. Bonaparte became profuse with apologies but it was all Barnes and Damer could do to quieten the excitable Hann.

Parents were well assured by the piety of Barnes's establishment, for his advertisement on returning to Dorchester had expressed the hope that his pupils would receive what should be 'the basis of all education – the Principles of Christian Piety'. Less orthodox was his attitude to punishment, for he never caned a boy, save in extreme cases of lying, and rarely upbraided his scholars. As a schoolmaster, Barnes attempted to appeal to the moral nature of his boys; in this he is fairly to be compared as a reformer to Thomas Arnold at Rugby who lay down a challenge to the habitual brutality of public school life by appealing to the higher motivation and Christian principles of his own boys.

In 1842, Barnes introduced into his school an instrument named the 'tropograph' which he used as a basis for his periodical reports on the scholars. It was no more in essence than a board with holes in it, and a number of pins by which the boys' progress could be charted through a series of colours. Barnes's real disciplinary weapon was, of course, the giving or withholding of his approval. The affection and regard in which his pupils held him was frequently attested in later life. They wrote to him and kept him aware of their progress.

One young lieutenant, who subsequently became a general, insisted that part of his first 'bag' of antelope heads, sent home

1. Watercolour portrait of a boy by William Barnes, thought to be a self-portrait.

2. (*Above left*): Ink and wash drawing of musicians by William Barnes.

3. (*Above right*): Detail from a portrait of John Barnes (1763-1846), the poet's father. Probably by John Thorne, dated 1838.

4. (*Below*): Engraving of Puncknowle Manor, near Bridport, by William Barnes, from the *Gentleman's Magazine*, July 1835.

5. (*Opposite page*): Julia Miles Barnes (1805-1852).

6. The Chantry House, Mere, in about 1830. Watercolour, probably by William Barnes.

7. Part of South Street, Dorchester, in about 1860. Norman House is the three storey building immediately beyond Napper's Mite (with clock).

8. (*Above*): William Barnes aged about fifty.

9. William Barnes in about 1870, from the portrait by G. Stuckey.

10. The Hon. Mrs Caroline Norton in about 1853, detail from a portrait by F. Stone.

11. Whitcombe Church. Barnes became its curate in 1847, and it was here he preached both his first and last sermons.

12. Winterborne Came Church. Barnes's grave is on the extreme left, under the trees.

13. The rectory, Winterborne Came.

14. William Barnes with friends and relatives at Winterborne Came rectory, October 1882. Barnes is seated third from left, William Miles Barnes is second from right, Laura Barnes extreme right.

15. William Barnes in old age, watercolour by John Leslie.

from a distant country, should go to his old schoolmaster to be part of the school museum. A young surgeon in South Africa, Frederick Ensor, was moved to write in admiration to his old schoolmaster after reading the *Poems of Rural Life* for the first time, on a 'hot steamy day on the east coast'. The poems brought vividly home to him the cool greenness of Dorset. Barnes, courteous as usual, replied to his old pupil and wrote again a little later to express his continuing interest.

Family life for the Barneses was a never-ending round of work and study, with Julia and Mrs Miles looking after the welfare of the fifteen to twenty-five boarders. Some of the parents demanded an unreasonable amount of attention, such as the mother who wrote to say that her son's head scurf should be brushed out regularly. The Barnes girls were educated at home with extra lessons in music and dancing from Frederick Smith. The two boys, who were born later, were educated in the school itself. Thus Julia was still engaged in the teaching of infants and young girls, and it is a credit to her thoroughness that her daughters gained the refinement and cultivation for which they were later noted. Barnes himself had a hand in their tuition in such subjects as modern languages, and, though his schemes for language teaching gained no general sway outside his own school, it is a matter of some note that each of his own six surviving children acquired some facility in three classical and three modern languages. The morning visitor to Norman House would have heard, as he was just about to enter, the clatter of plates from the kitchen below, the hum of voices from the schoolroom, and, perhaps, the strains of a pianoforte and a young girl's voice in an Italian aria, from the family apartments on the first floor. On summer afternoons the building was quieter, for Barnes would have walked out to Yellowham Wood with his boys, to look for botanical specimens, accompanied by his wife and children.

Few middle-class women of her time can have borne such a load of work so patiently as Julia. She was very economical in outlook and probably grudged paying for extra help in the house. Eventually they employed two maids, though the house was always understaffed by comparison with similar premises in the town. Barnes himself was never at ease as an employer. He disliked the hierarchical relationship which the custom of the time considered appropriate between a master and his servants. He was a considerate employer and rarely liked to trouble Maria Tizard and Jane Hall with the sort of requests that were elsewhere issued as orders. His daughters recalled that he would prefer to walk down the stairs with an empty coal scuttle rather than ring for the maid. When he did ask for something to be done, it was always uttered most gently: 'Oh Mary, *would* you be so kind as to give me some coals.'[8]

Shortly after the family's arrival in Dorchester, their infant son, Julius, died at the age of three. Barnes never seems to have mentioned the event to his other children when they grew up, and the only clear indication of it is a little receipt, pasted into his notebook, which reads:

> 'F Oliver. King's Arms Inn, Dorchester, 17 May 1837.
> pr. Horses for the Funeral of the
> late children of Mr Barnes. 10s 6d'[9]

The tender nature of William Barnes was apparent to all who knew him, and his inability to speak of his little son, or even to include him in the many tables of the family tree that he drew, can only be explained by the deep grief the tragedy must have caused him. But his silence found an outlet in two poems that are adequate memorials. In *To a Lost Child* he professed a longing for a time when death should no longer divide 'Thy face from mine', whilst in *Our Little Boy*, he evoked the character of the child:

> Since thou art gone, my lovely child, my dear
> Soon-wither'd flower, O let thy image flee
> From this bewilder'd mind, nor let me hear
> Thy lisping voice; nor feel thee on my knee.
> Where'er I turn my tearful eyes, I see
> Thy hands to play, thy face e'er smiling near.
> And Oh! thy smiles, that once were joy to me,
> Are touching now, and cost me each a tear.
> How long shall I, in idle dreams, embrace
> The air? How long shall thus my tearful sight
> Seem looking on the child I cannot see?
> Oh! that my closing eyes would hide thy face,
> Or see thy soul arising in the light.
> Full sweet would be a death for life with thee.[10]

The loss of Julius was partly assuaged by the birth of Isabel in 1838. Though she was a sickly child, she lived to the age of sixty-eight and died in 1906. Another son, William Miles, was born in March 1840, and, from the first, was treated as the true successor to his father. William Miles Barnes lived to the age of seventy-six and, for a time in later life, was Rector of Winterborne Monkton, a parish adjoining that of his father. The sixth and last surviving child, Egbert, was born at Norman's House in 1843 and died in 1877. Thus in the first nine years in Dorchester, the number of children in the family had increased from three to six while Julia herself had undergone four confinements.

All this weight of work was relieved by much pleasure and a real sense of fun in Barnes himself. His love of music was in no way diminished and the quartets, in which he loved to play at Mere, were now revived in Dorchester. The leading violin was, of course, Frederick Smith, with Thomas Patch at the 'cello and Mrs Bonifas at the piano. Barnes himself played second violin or flute. A number of such musical evenings were followed by a public concert at the Antelope Hotel which resulted in the formation of the Dorchester Philharmonic Society. Lucy Baxter recounted her memories of these evenings and those of hymn-singing at home:

'To this day the sound of music in the night awakens in some of them (WB's children) a rush of many childish memories. They also remember the more humble fireside music, when the children sat on their stools at their parent's feet, in the flickering firelight on a Sunday evening, and William Barnes and his wife sang hymns in which their shrill weaker trebles joined. The tiny children used to say, 'Father's voice was a big drum, and mother's like a flute.' On week-day evenings the husband and wife would sing duets such as 'Drink to me' and 'O Pescator dell' onda', etc. Sometimes the tiny children got the ascendant instead of the music, and then there were romps under and over father's knees, and a great scrambling of little dogs on all fours away from a great roaring bear who hunted them out, and when caught there were shrieks of half-frightened delight.'[11]

Barnes encouraged his children to play the games he had known in his own boyhood. He turned three tops on a lathe at Norman House, one for William, one for Egbert and one for himself. He had the faculty of becoming a child again and his good humoured laugh was a feature even of such solemn events as meetings of the county Archaeological Society in later years. He competed with his boys in their garret playroom as to who could keep a top spinning longest, and made time to romp with them. His children, in after life, could never remember a harsh word from him. Once he punished four of them by locking them in a room all day for refusing to admit to the breaking of an apple tree bough. The children played quite happily while their judge endured those same agonies known to Silas Marner when he locked Eppie in 'de toal hole'. Lucy Baxter later recalled the picture of utter remorse he presented when he released them from their captivity, having discovered the culprits among some of his scholars.

In 1846 his father, John, died and he lost his last close family connection with the Vale of Blackmore. Thereafter he tried to find a way of re-establishing the family link with the Vale but only succeeded some years later. In 1840, the friend of his youth, Edward Fuller, died at Staplegrove near Taunton. Fuller had suffered from consumption and his young wife had died a few months before him of the same complaint. He left William Barnes £100 to mark their friendship. Shortly after, Barnes wrote *The Music of the Dead*, a poem perhaps inspired by the knowledge that it was with Fuller he had first played in those far-off musical evenings in Dorchester:

> When music, in a heart that's true,
> Do kindle up wold loves anew,
> An' dim wet eyes, in feäirest lights,
> Do zee but inard fancy's zights;
> When creepen years, wi' with'ren blights,
>   'V a-took off them that wer so dear,
>   How touchen 'tis if we do hear
>   The tuens o' the dead, John. [12]

Barnes had always planned to take a trip to the Continent with Fuller, though, in his early days at Norman House he could not really have afforded the money or the time. Perhaps he put the £100 aside with the determination that one day he *would* go to France. He fulfilled his ambition in 1845 when the school broke up for the summer holidays. Trevor Hearl has deduced that he took the excursion from Poole to Le Havre on Friday 20 June, returning on the following Tuesday to Poole, crossing by the *S.S. Water-witch*, at a total cost of £1.[13] Dugdale mentions that Barnes visited Dieppe but, though this may have derived from family tradition there is no written record of it and Hearl is almost certainly correct. What is most curious for one who was to become a great linguist that of this, his only excursion to a foreign country, he left no commentary and there is not even a record of his spoken thoughts upon it. He may simply have hated the week-end, experienced acute *mâl-de-mer* or detested the continental Sunday. Perhaps things would have been different if he had had Edward Fuller with him to share the experience. The only item of interest resulting from the trip is a copy of his passport, issued at Le Havre and numbered 253, for it gives us an exact description of his appearance at the age of forty-five. We learn that his height was 5' 8", and that he had brown hair, blue eyes, a medium nose, a medium mouth, brown whiskers, a round chin and face and a 'usual' complexion.

While at Durngate Street he published nothing, but he began writing regularly at Norman House, perhaps because of the added convenience of his top-floor study. He wrote many of the Dorset dialect poems there, though none of his scholars nor, apparently, his family suspected that he was a poet. When the poems in the Dorset dialect were eventually published there was much speculation concerning their authorship, and it is significant that it was widely believed that the author was the radical contributor to *The Times*, Lord Sidney Godolphin. Barnes's public writing in the early years at Norman House consisted chiefly of contributions to the *Gentleman's Magazine* and a series of school text-books.

From 1837 to 1844 he wrote some seventeen articles for the *Magazine* and a number of reviews. Gough Nicholls the editor, sent Barnes review copies not only as an invitation to make his name as a scholar but also as a way of enlarging the library of this indigent schoolmaster. Despite such encouragement, many of the pieces are not much more than brief observations to 'Mr Urban' and all are couched in the style that was customary in the magazine. Whether long or short, profound or ephemeral, however, the articles are invariably clearly-written, logically argued and scrupulously researched. The tone is clearly that of a man who knows what he is talking about. The range of topics suggests an extraordinarily wide erudition and Nicholls must slowly have concluded that, in his contributor, he had something of a contemporary polymath. Barnes discussed with the readers such questions as: why the Gothic and Celtic races were different in their cultures; why people from all nations count in tens; who Aesop was; what were the exact dimensions of the Roman amphitheatre in Dorchester; how far the Phoenicians reached in their trade with the British Isles; the exact location of the battle of Penn; the ways in which the Dorset dialect resembled the tongue of the Anglo-Saxons. Sometimes the text would be illustrated by a woodcut made by the author, such as that of Fielding's House at East Stour, which appeared in the number for February 1841.

The commonest topics in these *Gentleman's Magazine* articles are philology and antiquarianism. Some are clearly developments of ideas that would have proved too complex for his pupils. Elsewhere in the *Magazine* articles are ideas which have a peculiar bearing upon pedagogy. An example of this is to be found in his piece upon Aesop where he observes that the human mind 'seems to delight in fable and allegorical teaching' – a tenet which influenced him both as a schoolmaster and poet. In later days, Barnes was quite happy to ransack these old articles for material for his new publications. Much of the Dissertation to his *Poems of Rural Life* first appeared as an article in the *Gentleman's Magazine*.

Perhaps the most remarkable of all these pieces were three that appeared in 1839 and 1840 on the beliefs of the Hindus. Barnes actually translated part of the Hindu 'Shasters' (or sacred books) and provided a commentary on them. He wrote on 'The Hindu Pooran and Sciences' and 'The Sects & Observances of Hindu Faqueers'. In writing on such subjects he was, no doubt, catering for a growing interest in the subject races of an imperial power but we may fairly ask how many other provincial schoolmasters could have done such a thing. He met that interest by reading and translating such a holy text as the *Ardeesh-i-mutifil* (or *The Ornament of the Assembly*). Furthermore, he was no mere translator, but one capable of communicating an intense excitement in the discovery of a religious tradition very different from the Victorian Episcopalians among whom he moved. He described

in some detail the customs of the Sunasees and the bodily priva-
tions and the dreadful tortures they endured to obtain the favour
of Brahma. In so doing, he engaged in an act of imaginative
sympathy which was rare at a time when the study of comparative religions had not been developed. With little tuition and
almost no research resources, he attempted to enter into remote
and alien cultures and to communicate his finds to the readers of
the *Magazine*. Pickard Cambridge once said of him that 'no
subject, no language daunted him once he made up his mind for
attack; his clear and logical understanding seemed to get hold of
a subject, take it in, absorb and assimilate it as completely as a
sea anemone does its food.'[15]

In the four years between 1839 and 1844 Barnes wrote six
school textbooks, and he published two more between 1844 and
1847. He may fairly be regarded as a pioneer in this field and,
furthermore, his textbooks give us a considerable insight into
his daily work as a schoolmaster. The books were:

1839 *A Corrective Concordance; or Imposition Book,*
1840 *An Arithmetical and Commercial Dictionary,*
1840 *An Investigation of the Laws of Case in Language,*
1841 *A Pronouncing and Etymological Dictionary of
Geographical Names,*
1842 *The Elements of English Grammar,*
1842 *The Elements of Linear Perspective and the
Projection of Shadows,*
1844 *Exercises in Practical Science,*
1847 *Outline of Geography and Ethnography for Youth.*

They were offered for sale by booksellers in Dorchester and
London, but with scant success and they were little used outside
his own school. The two features which make this series of little
books remarkable are, firstly, their logical and clear presentation
of the material and, secondly, the extraordinary range of subjects
with which they deal.

Barnes himself had enjoyed very little formal education.
Almost everything he knew he had had to teach himself from
books. He first taught himself a new subject and then, from his
notes, he taught the boys. The teaching notes he derived from
this exercise he would usually write up in the form of a textbook

for use in his own classes. His argument always proceeds from first principles by a series of logical steps and he had an Aristotelian dislike of an arbitrary assumption or an unexplained move in the argument. He believed that if boys were to retain knowledge they must be required to understand it thoroughly, rather than merely to commit it to memory. In this respect he may be regarded as an unusually-thoughtful teacher.

Much of his creative energies went into writing his textbooks, and they demonstrate how seriously he took his profession and how arduously he applied himself to it. A lot of his later writings tended to be polemical or explanatory, perhaps the reason why he wrote little poetry as he grew older. Few things are more likely to modify the subtlety of poetry than an urge to explain on the part of the poet and, for many years, it was Barnes's job to explain things all day long.

The titles of these little books give some notion of the range of subjects he taught and 'got up' for himself. His textbooks covered: Religious Education, Grammar, Arithmetic, Technical Drawing, Commerce, Geography and Science. The book on perspective he illustrated himself from his own wood blocks 'so as not to incur the expense of a professional.' The one characteristic they shared, despite their diversity, was that his approach was nearly always *verbal;* for him to teach a subject to his scholars was primarily to introduce them to the *vocabulary* of it. Nevertheless, he insisted upon the necessary relationship between words and their meanings in the education of his boys, taking them on walks throughout the surrounding countryside so that the vocabulary of trees, flowers, birds, fossils and earthworks became something to which they could attach associations.

In January 1841 he contributed an article to the *Gentleman's Magazine* in which he quoted some sentiments which had recently appeared in *Chambers' Edinburgh Journal:*

'We live too fast in the present age to spend so much time on WORDS. THINGS press upon us at every step, and an education dealing with THINGS, a *real* or reality education, as the Germans term it, is the education best fitted for the practical, the reality men, for the active classes of the community.'[16]

This article anticipated Gradgrind by thirteen years but the attitudes conveyed in it offended Barnes just as intensely as they would have annoyed Dickens. In the first place, he disapproved of the idea that an education in words was necessarily unpractical. He pointed out that a true education involved the development of concepts and experiences in the pupil's mind, so that the words should be meaningful, and argued that we must know the entire linguistic context of a word to comprehend it truly. Thus a Victorian schoolboy may translate the word 'toga' as 'cloak' but, if he does so, he will have an erroneous idea of how ancient Romans looked. Barnes's argument against the adequacy of translation, seems to be an answer to those who later urged him to 'transmute' his dialect poems into standard English:

'Since scholars know it to be impossible to make English versions of ancient works which could give a reader that knowledge of *things* which is carried in the works themselves, since no language but those which were formed to express those things can do so correctly.'

The *Arithmetical & Commercial Dictionary* is, as its name suggests, a glossary of terms and the list illustrates not only Barnes's wide general knowledge but also the kind of practical material he taught daily in his classroom. His boys would have learned that a GUILDER is 'A coin of Holland', value 5s.3d; that CULM is a type of stone coal found mainly in Wales; and that the derivation of the sign CWT is from the Latin 'centum', meaning one hundred, and the abbreviations 'wt' for weight. At times the reader will smile at the unconscious felicities of the list, as in the entry for CONSTANT which simply reads '(See Variable)'. Of the hundreds of questions, which must have echoed round the walls of Norman House, we may select:
W 'What is the daily income of an annuity of £146?' Ans.8s.
Q 'What will the hour figures of a clock amount to when added together? Ans.78.
Barnes rather enjoyed displaying his own curious lore in such texts as this. We should also remember that, despite his reputation for a dreamy disregard of all pecuniary matters, he was, by this time, something of a man of business himself and a successful one at that.
The most utopian of all his textbooks is *An Investigation of the*

Laws of Case in Language, which he advertised as no less than 'THE FIRST STEP TOWARDS A SYSTEM OF UNIVERSAL GRAMMAR.' His systematic mind investigated the similarities of case in over ten languages and found a patterning common to them which was not evident in the grammatical categorisations taught at the time. Consequently, this root and branch reformer proposed that, instead of the six cases of nouns commonly taught to schoolboys in Latin and Greek, nine should be put in their place. There is no evidence that his system was ever adopted outside his own school and, even in his own, no more is recorded of the teaching of the universal grammar. Perhaps even Barnes's schoolboys reacted against having to learn three more cases. Nevertheless, the linguistic attainments of his own children were such as to indicate that he must have employed novel methods of the teaching of languages to have achieved such extraordinarily successful results.

Much more orthodox was the *Elements of English Grammar* with its 112 pages neatly sectioned into comments on orthography, etymology, syntax and prosody. It is a conventional text, part of which might easily be found in use in schools today. It was the first of Barnes's books to be provided with an index and was presumably intended as a reference book for his scholars. From it they could have learned many a grammatical definition and also tested themselves by attempting to correct: 'The new piano forte is in the parlour, which mamma bought last week,' and 'I have seen the lady at the concert who sang so nicely at my Uncle's.' These grammatical examples provide us with an insight into the gentility of tone which was aimed at by Mr Barnes at his 'Academy'. The reality was probably more rowdy.

In 1837, Barnes put his name on the books of St John's College, Cambridge, as a 'ten years man'. He was therefore able to add to the title pages of his various school texts the words: 'by W. Barnes (of St John's College Cambridge). This is perhaps the nearest thing to a mild duplicity that Barnes ever engaged in, for the phrase would suggest that he was a *graduate* of the college, which, of course, he was not. He could have justifiably replied to such a charge that he nowhere falsely claimed a degree and that he was *of* St Johns, in the sense that he was a registered student there. Nevertheless, this description of himself must have helped him to gain recognition for his own scholarly authority and, perhaps, helped to sell a few copies more.

The book on linear perspective was written chiefly for use in his own school and the wooden blocks he cut to illustrate it are still on exhibition in the Dorset County Museum. Barnes's linguistic enthusiasm in no way precluded a passion for technical and scientific matters. His *Exercises in Practical Science* included sections on dynamics, statics, hydrostatics and hydrodynamics. It was described by the publisher as 'no bad introduction to Mechanical Science for those who may have to stand before the chair of a Professor.' Again he includes questions. 'What weight', he demands of the hapless schoolboy, 'will be upheld in water by a block of deal 2 feet thick, 3 feet broad, and 4 feet long, before it sink?'

The author made very little money from all this publication. Years later he wrote a characteristically humorous anecdote for *Macmillan's Magazine:*

'We have known of one strong case of plagiarism from the labours of a man whom we will call A, and who had printed a small book for his own use as a teacher. Some years afterwards he received from a friend of his, B, at a distance, a manuscript, which he, B, told him had just been written by a friend of his C, for his use as a teacher, and that he, C, meant to print it, but had submitted it to him, B, for his corrective perusal, and that he, B, should like to know A's opinion of it. A found it to be a *verbatim* copy of his own little book; and the answer he sent to B was to the effect that he could not recommend C to print it for gain, since he himself had already printed it, and it had not yielded him a shilling profit.'[17]

Barnes's growing interest in antiquarian matters was given practical expression in 1845 by the foundation of the Dorset County Museum and Library. This event was brought about by the publication of plans proposing suggested routes for the first railway lines into Dorset. A broad-gauge line was planned to run from Yeovil, while the 'corkscrew' line was projected from Southampton. Between 1845 and the final arrival of the railway into Dorchester on June 1, 1847, antiquarian opinion was firstly alarmed by the possible damage done to the county's ancient monuments, and then organised to minimise it. In Dorchester itself, concern was felt about the survival of the Roman amphitheatre known as 'Maumbury Ring' and of Poundbury, the large earthwork to the north-west of the town. Barnes was himself enthusiastic about the railways but also feared the damage they might do. With two like-minded friends, the Reverend Charles Bingham and the antiquary, Charles Warne, he alerted the Archaeological Association so that pressure was brought to bear on the railway companies. The London & South Western Railway was persuaded to alter the angle of its projected line from Dorchester to Weymouth so that it passed some yards to the south-east of Maumbury; the Great Western Railway was similarly induced to run its line a little to the west of the amphitheatre. Barnes was also involved in saving Poundbury, by persuading the Great Western Railway to agree to tunnel under the earthworks rather than through it.

So much lobbying required an organisation. On 15 October, 1845 an inaugural meeting at the Antelope Hotel agreed to found a County Museum and Library. The Right Honourable Lord Ashley, MP, subsequently famous as the reforming 7th Earl of Shaftesbury, was elected President. The Hon Treasurer was to be Mr Herbert Williams, and the two Hon Secretaries were the Rev C.W. Bingham and Barnes himself. He thus became a founder member of the Dorset Natural History and Field Club (later the Dorset Natural History and Archaeological Society), which maintains the Museum to this day. As secretary, Barnes became officially responsible for establishing a collection of antiquities and also for preserving the historic sites throughout the county. A starting point came with the collections made by his scholars over the years. The Museum was first established at Judge Jeffrey's House in High West Street, was then moved to some rooms behind the Antelope Hotel, and finally opened its doors at the junction of High West Street and Cornmarket in 1881, on which site it is still housed.[18]

The secretaryship gave Barnes an excellent opportunity to extend his knowledge of antiquities and, in time, he became locally famous for his scholarshp. Two incidents especially impressed his fellow townsmen. The first is recollected in *Ancient Britain*, which first appeared in 1858. It seems that a local dentist, named Maclean, opened some local barrows in order to examine the teeth of the skeletons contained within them. In

one barrow, the skeletons' remains were associated with a quan-
tity of 'hard brittle stuff' which puzzled Maclean. When he
consulted Barnes, the schoolmaster, drawing upon his years of
gardening experience at Mere, identified the material as rasp-
berry seeds. Some of the seeds were given to a local gardener
named Hartweg to plant and, of the six he received, three
actually sprouted. Such a result would have amazed his contemporaries but they were, no doubt, equally impressed with
Barnes's solution to another puzzle which had troubled local
historians. Large quantities of pierced shale discs had been
found in the area of Kimmeridge and there had been speculation
that such objects may have been used as coins by the ancient
Britons. From his years of work with a lathe, Barnes offered the
view that these curious pieces were turnings from a lathe 'used
on the spot at some remote time, in turning vessels or ornaments
for which there was then a considerable demand.'[19] Recent
examinations have tended to support his opinion. It is worth
noticing that these two identifications, which much increased
Barnes's reputation as the antiquarian, were based not upon
obscure reading but the practical pastimes he cultivated at Mere.

Such local successes as these must have endowed even the
cautious Barnes with a degree of confidence in his future prospects. His family was established as a respectable part of Dorchester society; his school was prospering; his reputation as an
author and antiquarian was growing both locally and nationally.
Furthermore, a book of dialect poems he had published in 1844
had earned him the attention of literary London.[20] He had also
gone a fair way in his studies for a degree at Cambridge University and was confidently looking forward to ordination as a
clergyman of the Church of England. Though a Blackmore boy of
the humblest origins, had he not, by hard work and study,
shown himself to be worthy of high pedagogic office as much as
any gentleman-born Oxford graduate? The Dorchester establishment did not need to think long about the question. Its answer
was 'No'.

In May 1846 Richard Cutler resigned as Headmaster of
Hardye's Grammar School. Barnes confidently applied for the
post, thinking perhaps that, in the case of appointment he would
close his own school or, perhaps, run the two in tandem. Hardye's

was an 'endowed' school and, therefore, more financially secure than his own, especially at a time when the repeal of the Corn Laws looked as if it might undermine the economy of rural towns such as Dorchester. Barnes's letter of application to the 'Feoffees', or governors, was supported by two petitions, both signed by townsmen of good reputation. The first contained twenty-seven signatures, and the second, seventy-eight. In addition he had the support of Richard Brinsley Sheridan of Frampton House and other local notables. John Gough Nicholls, the eminent editor of the *Gentleman's Magazine*, wrote a letter of support, while the Reverend John Colson, of St Peter's, Dorchester, expressed his 'high opinion' of Barnes's 'religious and moral character'. One of the most influential landowners, Colonel Damer of Came, whose own son had been a pupil at Norman House, declared in a letter that 'Mr Barnes ... (was) ... a very intelligent highly (proficient?) and intellectual gentleman.

The Feofees were due to meet on 30 May under their Chairman, the Earl of Shaftesbury. Before the meeting it became known that the committee (probably its chairman) preferred to adhere to their tradition of appointing a man in orders. Barnes probably felt little concern on that account because it was common knowledge that he was to be ordained, as, indeed, he was in the following February. On the morning of the meeting, however, it was circulated in the town that the Feofees were insisting that the successful candidate should *already* be in holy orders. This put a finish to his hopes. He recorded the matter tersely in his notebook: 'This year I was a candidate for the Headmastership of Dorchester Grammar School and some votes but fewer than Mr Maskew, who was chose, the 30th May, 1846.'

The reasons for his rejection are still a matter of speculation. He was not a grammar school man himself; he was not yet a university graduate; he had at one time been a clerk in the town and was even reputed to be descended from farm labourers. He was also an eccentric and persisted in wearing an old blue dressing gown while teaching. He had of late published some dialect poems, an act not fitting the dignity of the Headmaster of such a school as Hardye's. It was perhaps this sort of social argument that had sounded round the walls in the Feoffees' meeting room. It may have been that the arguments were a little more political.

Had not he written a Dissertation to his poems which the radical Sherborne newspaper had interpreted as a reproach to land-lords? It was obvious that he was not politically sound. Why, he would not even put his own maidservants in their places. It was clearly safer to appoint the Reverend Ratsey Maskew of Swyre, a prizeman of Trinity College, Cambridge, and the author of *Annotations on the Acts of the Apostles.*[21]

Barnes's failure to obtain the headship did his own reputation serious damage. Those who had supported him so confidently felt slightly let down. Perhaps the Feoffees knew something detrimental to their man that they did not know. Moreover, Barnes had secured an enemy in Simonds, the editor of *The Dorset County Chronicle*, who had shown little sympathy for him. Barnes retorted by cancelling the *Chronicle* and Simonds replied by sending him an additional bill for the printing of the Dorset dialect poems. Barnes rejected the extra charge and there the matter stood for a number of years. The dispute was particularly damaging to Barnes's interests because Simonds was not only the printer of his poems but also the editor of the most effective organ for advertisements in the county. In publicising a school, the *Fashionable Guide* was no substitute for the *Chronicle*.

In all, it was the most bitter blow of Barnes's professional life. He had always believed in the virtues of hard-work and self-help, and assumed that patient merit would inevitably find recognition and reward. Now he knew that he was wrong. His response was simply to try to shrug off the disappointment and to turn once again to the consolations of home and scholarship. His temperament was naturally that of a quietist but the hurt done to him was none the less painful for all his lack of indigna-tion.

A man unsure of his position in society may turn for consola-tion either to God or Mammon. For some time before his rejec-tion by the Hardye Feoffees, Barnes had sought security in both and, in the mid 1840's was already on his way to becoming a man of God and a man of property. For many years he had been painfully conscious of his anomalous position as a would-be scholar who was not even a graduate. In 1836, the Reverend Cassan had persuaded him to apply for entry to Oxford Univer-sity but he had been rejected. But his registration as a 'ten year man' at St John's College, Cambridge, in 1838, meant that he might study for the degree of a Bachelor of Divinity. The course entailed ten years of part-time study at home, as well as the keeping of prescribed terms in college before the final examinations. In June 1847 he left his school early in the term to the keeping of Julia and Hann, so that he might keep a term at St John's. On June 4 he was engaged in preparing a Latin sermon and a little later he preached a sermon in St Mary's Church, before the Vice Chancellor of the University and the Regius Professor of Divinity. The result was apparently satisfactory because he was afterwards invited to tea with his tutor.

For the first time in his life he was mixing daily with men of equal intellect, and his letters to Julia reveal his delight. He wrote: 'I have made the acquaintance of another of our men who paints admirably, and is a good musician; he has introduced me to a friend of his at Queen's College, who is learned in architecture. There are certainly many superior minds here.' On July 6, for the first and only time in his life, he saw Queen Victoria, when he was one of a crowd of two thousand students gathered in Trinity College to greet her on the installation of Prince Albert as Chancellor of the University.

'I went in', he scribbled to Julia, 'with an impetuous wave that carried everything before it; and in which doctors with their red robes were pushed into scarecrows, and masters had their hoods torn off, and your unworthy admirer got his silver chain broken.'[22] His enjoyment of Cambridge days was diminished by his recurring worries about Julia. His absence threw much more work and responsibility onto her, and he was concerned about her health. Yet he now began to regard the winning of his degree as an essential step to ensure his own professional fortunes and, therefore, indirectly, the prosperity of his wife and family.

He had also made preparations to be ordained. In the first years after his return to Dorchester, he had served as a voluntary district visitor and his help to the poor had been noted by John Colson, the Rector of St Peter's, who had then advised him to consider taking orders. In 1843-4 he had also acted as the people's warden at St Peter's. In order to be ordained, he needed supporters of some influence in the church who would be prepared to underwrite his application. In January 1847 he received a considerable assurance of support when Colonel Damer, his old friend, presented him with the donative of Whitcombe, which had carried a stipend of £13 a year since the time of Henry VIII. Whitcombe was a donative – which means something less than a curacy – within the parish of Winterborne Came. When Damer made his offer, Barnes was only a deacon and, strictly speaking, no form of living could be accepted by one not yet in Holy Orders. The Rector of Winterborne Came, the Reverend George Arden, had already been very helpful in the matter by willingly relinquishing the £13 for Whitcombe, which was part of his own parish. He now tried to help in another way by suggesting to the Bishop that Barnes should become his curate at Whitcombe, and therefore entitled to the donative. But the Bishop of Salisbury decided to make a special case of Barnes and formally to regard the gift of Damer's as Barnes's entitlement to orders.[23]

It was still necessary for Barnes to be successful in the ordination examinations and he presented himself to be examined at Salisbury on February 24 1847. He was required to write an English sermon on a given text, and then to translate a long passage of Hooker into Latin. The first hurdle was successfully cleared and, on 28 February, William Barnes was ordained as a clergyman of the Church of England. He returned from Salisbury to Wool by the new railway line and was met by Julia and the older children. A change in title often changes the way in which a man regards himself. Henceforth the Reverend William Barnes progressively discarded his old blue dressing gown and adopted the more standard clerical dress. Each Sunday morning, he walked three miles out of Dorchester on the Broadmayne Road, to conduct the service at Whitcombe. He had begun a Christian ministry which was to last for the rest of his long life.

Meanwhile the school continued to thrive under Julia's careful household management and, for the first time in his life, Barnes found that he had saved a large sum of money. Trevor Hearl has estimated that, by 1845, he had saved about £1000. In that year the income of the school was about £1000, whereas the accounts show only £378.18s.6d as outgoings, though this did not include the salaries of the ushers and other expenses.[24] For some years Barnes had been lending out money at interest. That he was a charitable and understanding creditor is witnessed by the letter from a Mrs Harris which he received from the Blackmore Vale in May. She expressed her gratitude that, in her recent widow-hood, he had not pressed her for payment of interest, but assures him that he will received £100 soon. Another borrower was his old friend Richard Carey, who wrote to request £600 in 1845.

Since his father's death in 1846, Barnes had looked for a way of re-establishing the family name in the Vale. His old employers, the solicitors, Messrs Dashwood, were asked to try to find some local property for him as an investment. His notes for 1847 record the result of their search: 'This year £300 of which I had lent at mortgage at Sturminster Newton was paid off and I bought Creedman's & Mogg's Mead at Sturminster for £360.' The money was probably from Mrs Harris. These two fields lay on either side of the River Stour. He celebrated the purchase by the poem *The Pleace Our Own Again,* the first verse of which is a tribute to Julia's (or 'Jeane's') economy, which had made the purchase possible:

> Well! thanks to you, my faithvul Jeane,
> So worksome wi' your head an' hand,
> We seaved enough to get agean
> My poor vorefather's plot o' land.
> 'Twer folly lost, an cunnen got,
> What should ha' come to me by lot,
> But let that goo; 'tis well the land
> Is come to hand, by be'th or not.'[25]

These fields were not exactly those owned by his father but that did not mar his feeling of satisfaction. They were let out to a Vale farmer, James Rose, whose rich Blackmore talk was a source of delight to Barnes for many years to come. Rose would send Barnes his rental of six guineas per half year by cutting the notes in half and sending the two parts in different envelopes. Only once did they disagree, when Rose wanted to pollard the elms by the river to 'tidy them up.' Barnes's refusal on aesthetic grounds was a continual source of puzzlement to him. Barnes's attitude in this matter may have influenced that of Thomas Hardy, who refused to have the trees lopped or thinned round his home at Max Gate.

In 1847, Barnes made an even more important purchase. His
school was full to bursting. He needed a yet larger set of premises
and eventually secured them on the western side of South Street
at a house formerly belonging to Mr Hawkins. He purchased the
lifehold for £700 and with it, one of the best sites in Dorchester.
No matter that the recent repeal of the Corn Laws had cast a
shadow over the rural economy. With Julia's help he could pros-
per in such a place.

6

Poems of Rural Life
1844-1846

The culmination of Barnes's life as a poet came as early as 1844 when the *Poems of Rural Life in the Dorset Dialect* was first published. Though he was to write much more poetry, and was to make second and third collections of his 'Hwomely Rhymes', the nature and range of his art as a dialect poet was substantially established by 1844. The first edition ran to 373 pages of which 240 were devoted to the dialect poems, but they were sandwiched between a 37 page Dissertation and nearly 100 pages headed 'A Glossary of the Dorset Dialect of the English Language.' Every page bespeaks a profound and an original mind, which combines a knowledge of curious lore with a deep familiarity with the life and language of Blackmore people.

The spirit of the book was antagonistic to that of the age. In a year which saw the publication of Chambers' *Vestiges of Creation* the poems celebrate ancient pieties. While Thomas Cook was planning his first travel excursions Barnes's poems depict the merits of a settled community. While Bradshaw issued his *Railway Guide* and the network of track stretched out to the borders of Dorset itself, the scale of Barnes's concerns is that of the distances people could walk. His themes are those of hearth, home and rural customs. Much of the material would have seemed absurdly antiquated to the new men of the age, for whom the steam engine was transforming the dimensions of life.

In the Preface to the second edition of the *Lyrical Ballads* in 1800, Wordsworth expressed his concern at the effects of the new sensationalist publications upon rural communities. He observed that a 'multitude of causes, unknown to former times ... (was) ... now acting with a combined force to blunt the discriminating powers of the mind.' The opening words of the Dissertation to the *Poems of Rural Life in the Dorset Dialect* echo some of Wordsworth's concern. But it quickly becomes apparent that Barnes is not offering his poetry as some sort of therapy for the treatment of cases of exposure to mass media, as Wordsworth was. Rather was he engaged upon the task of linguistic conservation:

'As increasing communication among the inhabitants of different parts of England, and the spread of school education among the lower ranks of our population, tend to substitute book-English for the provincial dialects, it is likely that after a few years many of them will linger only in the more secluded parts of the land, if they live at all; though they would give valuable light to the antiquary as well as the philologist, of that increasing class who wish to purify our tongue and enrich it from its own resources.'[1]

Poems are normally offered to the public as items of intrinsic aesthetic interest. Barnes's Dissertation casts doubt upon his primary intentions in presenting the poems; are they to be regarded as works of art, or merely as specimens of a language artificially preserved in poetic form for the benefit of the antiquarian and philologist? There can be no doubt that a number of readers regarded the book chiefly as a repository of rural phrase and expression for, on May 7 1844, John Russell Smith, the London publisher of the book, wrote to Barnes to observe that he had not yet sold many copies and that 'those who want only the Glossary and Dissertation think 10/- too much.' There is, in the Dorset County Museum, a second edition of the book with the Glossary removed. The early philological readers thought of the poems as no more than illustrations of the usage of words explained in the Glossary and of the linguistic theories outlined in the Dissertation. To readers interested in poetry, the Glossary was no more than necessary footnotes to the poems.

Neither view is adequate. The originality of the *Poems of Rural Life in the Dorset Dialect* lies in the fact that art and scholarship are related in its pages. The book combines Barnes's growing interest in philology with his quick observation, with ear and eye, of Dorset life. It unites his total seriousness of purpose with his buoyant sense of humour; his knowledge of ancient tongues with his familiarity with the vernacular. It is at once erudite and popular, esoteric and homely, and is, therefore, a just image of the idiosyncratic mind that produced it.

The Dissertation is a curious amalgam of history, philology and poetics in which Barnes traces the history of the West Saxons from whose language he believed the Dorset dialect to be derived. He claims for the dialect that it is 'a broad and bold shape of the English language, as the Doric was of the Greek'. It is 'rich in humour, strong in raillery and hyperbole; and, altogether, as fit a vehicle of rustic feeling and thought, as the Doric is found in the *Idyllia* of Theocritus'. Barnes is especially dismissive of those who consider the dialect to be a corruption of written English. Dorset, he argued, was richer and purer than 'that dialect which has been chosen as the national speech', purer in that it employed many words from the Saxon while English coined new names from foreign tongues, richer in that Dorset had names for many things which, in English, could only be referred to by the use of an entire phrase.

Barnes develops his argument by the suggestion, familiar from his *Gentleman's Magazine* pieces, that French expressions such as 'tout ensemble' and 'coup-de-grace' along with all other 'continental phraseology' should be rejected in favour of words formed from the native stock. As an example he points out that the name of the plant 'sorrel' has been formed from the word 'sour' because of the nature of the plant. Thus the poems themselves became demonstrations of the range of expression available in the dialect and, therefore, the indigenous Saxon speech forms.

When the first of his Dorset poems had appeared in *The Dorset County Chronicle* they had been regarded by their readers as jokes. Not only was the local speech a matter for amusement but the farm-worker himself was an object of ridicule to those who took their words and ways from genteel urban sources. Nearly forty years after the publication of Barnes's book, Thomas Hardy was still defending the Dorsetshire labourer against those who regarded him as a comic 'Hodge', a 'degraded being of uncouth manner and aspect, stolid understanding, and snail-like movement.'[2] It is true that Barnes in these poems delights in the verbal humour of his rustics but he laughs with them and not at them. The Dorset dialect is for him the medium of humour not the object of it. His characters are often amusing because they are strong in raillery, not because they are intrinsically ridiculous either as farm labourers or as dialect speakers.

Furthermore, the poems are not merely written *about* Dorset people, he claims to be writing *for* them. His audience, he says, is not cast among those with town occupations. The poems are offered to 'the happy mind of the milkmaid with her cow, or the dairy farmer's son in the hayfield' or 'the innocent evening cheerfulness of the family circle on the stone floor.' Even in 1844, however, he cannot resist a note of Victorian moralising by adding that the poems are 'free of slang or vice' and strive chiefly to utter the 'happy emotions' with which the mind contemplates the 'charms of rural nature'. Some readers may have noticed a contradiction between the determination to write *for* the rural audience and the provision of a Glossary of their language. Barnes probably hoped to be read among his fellow Dorset men and women but included the scholarly apparatus both to bolster the claims of the poems to be worthy of publicaton, and to appeal to a select circle of genteel and even academic readers.

None of the poems bears on any part of his life after he left Blackmore in 1818. It is as if he had subconsciously decided that only the earliest portion of his life – with the brief exception of his courting of Julia – was worth writing about. There are no poems about the life of a clerk in a provincial town, his work as a schoolmaster for forty years or his later life as pastor to a country flock. It is Blackmore that made him a poet and it is from recollections of Vale life that he took his subject matter. The whole of his adult life was an experience in prose. His debt to the Vale of Blackmore and its people is made quite explicit in his Dissertation to the poems, which, he says, 'are written from the associations of an early youth that was passed among rural families in a secluded part of the county'. With a rather selective memory he praises the 'sound Christian principles, kindness and harmless cheerfulness' of the people he represents. He is more accurate concerning the language of the poems:

'The dialect in which he (the poet) writes is spoken in its greatest purity in the villages and hamlets of the secluded and beautiful Vale of Blackmore.'[3]

The *Poems of Rural Life in the Dorset Dialect* was first published in the spring of 1844 by John Russell Smith of London and George Simonds of Dorchester. A second edition appeared in

1847[3], corrected and expanded to 411 pages. The title page bore
an epigraph from Columella and the scholarly appearance of the
book was designed to reassure the reader that it was not the work
of an unlettered ploughboy. The poems were arranged in a
seasonal scheme: Spring, Summer, Fall and Winter, perhaps,
influenced by such works as John Clare's *The Shepherd's Calendar*
which appeared in 1827. Not all the poems fitted easily into the
frame and Barnes was obliged to include a fifth section entitled
'Miscellaneous Pieces' in the first edition. Interestingly, by 1847
and the second edition, Barnes was progressively more teutonic
in thought so that the final section was then named 'Sundry
Pieces'. The first reviewer in *The Dorset County Chronicle* picked
up Barnes's philological intentions by observing that readers of
the poems in his newspaper had eagerly turned to 'Poet's Corner'
to enjoy 'another tit-bit in their own native Saxon tongue.'[5]

Because Barnes chose dialect poetry for his medium, there is
always, in these poems, the sound of a speaking voice and,
therefore, of human personality and dramatic situation. Sometimes we are able to identify the name, sex and age of the speaker
but at times we have to fill in the details from our own imagination. Even when the identity of the speaker is shadowy, however, there is always a point of view taken and expressed with a
vigorous sense of the appreciation of life. An example is to be
found in *Bob the Fiddler:*

> Oh! Bob the fiddler is the pride
> O' chaps an' maïdens vur an' wide;
> They can't keep up a merry tide,
>   But Bob is in the middle.
> If merry Bob do come avore ye,
> He'll zing a zong, or tell a story;
> But if you'd zee en in his glory,
>   Jist let en have a fiddle.
>
> Aye, let en tuck a crowd below
> His chin, an' gi'e his vist a bow,
> He'll dreve his elbow to an' fro',
>   An' plaÿ what you do please.
> At Maÿpolen, or feäst, or feäir,
> His eärm wull zet off twenty peäir,
> An' meäke em dance the groun' dirt-beäre,
>   An' hop about lik' vlees.[6]

In many of Barnes's poems the true object of attention is not the apparent topic – in this case Bob himself – but the character of the speaker. As readers we must imagine a situation, perhaps a chance reference to Bob, or perhaps an actual performance which we attend, when an old admirer, perhaps some old labourer with his alepot, insists on buttonholing us so that he may pour the praises of Bob into our ears. The energy and vigour of the account re-enacts the stamping boisterousness of many a country 'randy' where Bob has played. When we read the poem we remember that, for hundreds of years, remote rural communities were entirely dependent upon itinerant fiddlers for social music. Both Thomas Hardy and his father walked the country roads to fiddle at local 'tides'.

The *Poems of Rural Life* contain many such portraits of country people: Moll Brown, the witch who lives along the lane; Uncle and Aunt; 'Grammar' telling tales to the children while musing over her old shoes; faithless Jeane of Grenley Mill. Each poem is animated by the attitude of the narrator, whether it be one of censure, affectionate recollection, or personal grief. Each character is placed firmly in the context of country life so that, to read the poems is to sketch in an entire village community of pre-enclosure times.

The seasonal frame Barnes chooses for the poems ensures that a full record is presented of the various times of the country calendar. There are poems of Eastertime and 'club-walking' at Whitsun; of hay-making, thatching, mowing, harvest-time, Guy Fawkes night and Christmas revels; there are incidents from country life: such as driving the common, consulting gypsies for predictions, playing ghosts in the moonlit threshing floor and going to Shrodon Fair. The folk-history preserved in the poems is sometimes rendered in meticulous detail. In *Leady-Day, an' Ridden House*, for example, we learn exactly how a wagon was packed with the family's household goods, when the farmworker moved to another farm:

> Well, zoo, avore the east begun
> To redden wi' the comen zun,
> We left the beds our mossy thatch
> Wer never mwore to overstratch,
> An' borrow'd uncle's wold hoss *Dragon*,

To bring the slowly lumbren waggon,
An' when he come, we vell a-packen
The bedsteads, wi' their rwopes an' zacken;
An' then put up the wold eärm-chair,
An' cwoffer vull ov e'then-ware,
An' vier-dogs, an' copper kittle,
Wi' crocks an' saucepans, big an' little;
An' fryen-pan, vor aggs to slide
In butter round his hissen zide,
An' gridire's even bars, to bear
The drippen steäke above the gleäre
O' brightly-glowen coals. An' then
All up o' top o' them ageän
The woaken bwoard, where we did eat
Our croust o' bread or bit o' meat,-
An' when the bwoard wer up, we tied
Upon the reäves, along the zide,
The woaken stools, his glossy meätes,
Bwoth when he's beäre, or when the pleätes
Do clatter loud wi' knives, below
Our merry feäces in a row;
An' put between his lags, turn'd up'ard,
The zalt-box an' the corner cupb'ard.
An' then we laid the wold clock-ceäse,
All dumb, athirt upon his feäce,
Vor we'd a-left, I needen tell ye,
Noo works 'ithin his head or belly.
An' then we put upon the pack
The settle, flat upon his back;
An' after that, a-tied in pairs
In woone another, all the chairs,
An' bits o' lumber wo'th a ride,
An, at the very top a-tied,
The children's little stools did lie,
Wi' lags a-turn'd toward the sky:[7]

Because Barnes was reworking the memories of a quarter of a century past, a prevailing theme of the poems is that of reminiscence and a common tone that of nostalgia. Memories could be re-awakened in him by a familiar landscape, a well-loved name or a commonplace object such as an old wagon. Indeed, in the poem *The Wold Waggon* he not only described in detail the appearance of the wagon itself, but recalled the diverse characters of the horses that pulled them:

> Upon his head an' tail wer pinks,
> A-païnted all in tangled links;
> His two long zides wer blue, — his bed
> Bent slightly upward at the head;
> His reäves rose upward in a bow
> Above the slow hind-wheels below.
> Vour hosses wer a-kept to pull
> The girt wold waggon when 'twer vull:
> The black meäre *Smiler*, strong enough
> To pull a house down by herzuf,
> So big, as took my widest strides
> To straddle halfway down her zides;
> An' champen *Vi'let*, sprack an' light,
> That foam'd an' pull'd wi' all her might:
> An' *Whitevoot*, leäzy in the treäce,
> Wi' cunnen looks an' snow-whîte feäce;[8]

Like Hardcastle in *She Stoops to Conquer*, Barnes loved things that were old, 'old friends, old times, old books', though not old wines for he was an abstemious man. He disliked new-fangled inventions and in the poem *The Settle and the Girt Wood Vire*, the speaker, who is an old man, confides to a crony how much he prefers the settle and open fire to the more modern sofa, armchairs with their anti-macassars, and the small Victorian fire-grates. In *Woak were good enough Woonce*, Barnes declares in favour of furniture made from native wood to that fashioned from imported mahogany. The elegiac note in his poetry is most often heard in memoirs of old friends and old times, in the faces and the voices that are gone:

> What tender thoughts do touch woone's soul,
>   When we do zee a meäd or hill
> Where we did work, or plaÿ, or stroll,
>   An' talk wi' vaïces that be still;
> 'Tis touchen vor to treäce, John,
> Wold times drough ev'ry pleäce, John;
>   But that can't touch woone's heart so much,
> As zome wold long-lost feäce, John.[9]

Barnes's poems have been celebrated chiefly for their love of nature and descriptions of trees, flowers and river-side scenes. Though these things are important in the poems, they are made so because each natural object evokes human associations and memories in the poet. The accuracy of Barnes's descriptions of natural history cannot be compared to that of a poet such as Clare. Barnes's primary interests are human and dramatic, as in the tale of Meary-Ann's child who dies in the night, in the story of the beam in Grenley Church which was placed there overnight by a mysterious workman, in the political eclogues, and in the humorous poems such as *A Bit O' Sly Coortin* – a popular favou-rite when he came to give readings of his poems.[10]

Yet Barnes himself preferred his 'pathetic' poems to his comic ones. Many of these treat of the loss of the loved one through death or other cases. Such poems poignantly anticipate the death of Julia Miles and it may be that her recurrent illnesses led Barnes to assuage his dread of her death by incorporating it into his verse.

The Dorset poems exhibit a considerable amount of technical variation in rhyme scheme, stanza form and parallelisms. The early eclogues which are included in the *Poems of Rural Life* are written in iambic tetrameter, as also are the 'folk' poems such as *Leady-Day, an' Ridden House'* and *The Wold Wagon*. These poems are invariably cast in rhymed couplets which enabled Barnes to add afterthoughts and little touches of detail if he wanted to, but render them repetitive in the development of their thought and rather abrupt and inconsequential in their endings.

Barnes's studies in philology brought new variations to his writing, however, and his readings in other languages did not omit a study of their poetry. Astonishingly, this English dialect poet, who had never been abroad nor learned a foreign language in school or university, began to employ poetic devices culled from many languages. William Turner Levy has identified in his work such effects as the Norse half-rhyme or 'skot-hending', the Persian 'eekfa' or vowel rhyme, the Irish 'cumharda' or corres-pondence device, the Welsh 'cynghanedd', and many other such figures as well as the more familiar chiasmus and alliteration.[11] An examination of his finest poetry does indeed reveal a com-plexity of crafting which is probably unsuspected by the casual reader:

EVENEN IN THE VILLAGE

Now the light o' the west is a-turn'd to gloom,
  An' the men be at hwome vrom ground;
An' the bells be a-zenden all down the Coombe
  From tower, their mwoansome sound.
    An' the wind is still,
    An' the house-dogs do bark,
An' the rooks be a-vled to the elems high an' dark,
    An' the water do roar at mill.

An' the flickeren light drough the window-peäne
  Vrom the candle's dull fleäme do shoot,
An' young Jemmy the smith is a-gone down leäne,
  A-plaÿen his shrill-vaïced flute.
    An' the miller's man
    Do zit down at his ease
On the seat that is under the cluster o' trees,
    Wi' his pipe an' his cider can. [12]

The language of this poem is endearingly homely ('at hwome
vrom ground') and the sharpness of observation of such things
as the height and darkness of the elms and the exact tone of
Jemmy's flute are perfectly judged. But the delicacy of this poem
and its fineness of perception are products of its intricate stanzaic form and its almost unnoticed rhyme-schemes. In each verse
the latter four lines are so paced as to slow down the verse so that
the echoes and images they evoke can settle into our minds.
There are lovely undulations of the chain-rhymes such as
'peane', 'fleame', 'leane' and 'A-playen'. Thomas Hardy thought
that though Barnes was 'Primarily spontaneous, he was academic closely after' and concluded that 'he (Barnes) would at
times allow art to overpower spontaneity'. Not even in Burns
was there 'such searchings for the most cunning syllables.' [13]
Geoffrey Grigson went further than this by arguing that far from
being a 'spontaneous act', Barnes's writing of dialect poetry was
a product of his philological studies; it was 'a learned perversity'
which once attempted he found he could do by nature. [14] In fact,
the early eclogues precede his serious philological enquiry. As
we have seen in *Evenen in the Village* it is the combination of the
apparent naïvete of dialect with the subtlety of stanzaic and

rhyme effects which endows his verse with its most characteristic note.

The *Poems of Rural Life* were immediately successful with local critics in Dorset. *The Dorset County Chronicle*, in which they had first appeared – some in the agricultural columns, others in 'Poet's Corner' – naturally gave them considerable attention and, with almost parental pride, offered two long reviews on 16 May, just after the book came out, and again on 16 October 1844:

'this is real poetry, a description so full of truth and feeling that each resident in the county will at once fancy it the picture of his own home, every line conveying to his own mind what he sees, hears and feels in his evening walk through the village at this time of year.'

The *Chronicle* reviewer regarded the poems chiefly as exhortations to contentment and respectability: 'the poems of Mr Barnes are free of any coarse vulgarity and urge the village labourer in the words of Bishop Hacket to 'Fear God and be cheerful'.' The October review takes the odd notion that not even 'the warmest admirers of Dorset will . . . claim for it any characteristic share of beauty.' Deprived of the Wordsworthian beauties of mountain, lake and forest, Barnes had the more difficult task to find pleasure in more gentle scenery.[14]

The *Chronicle* reviewer considered that Barnes had successfully employed language in producing 'a series of portraits of which (though we never saw the individuals) we seem to know the originals.' In case there should be any doubt about the social and political implications of the poems the *Chronicle* repeated its view that the chief effect of the verses was to enjoin the peasant reader to obedience and contentment and to place the blessings of his position before the man who: 'was, perhaps, before, hardly conscious how many were the advantages he possessed: he was not alive to the real dignity of his simple position.'[15]

The *Chronicle's* radical rival, the *Sherborne and Yeovil Mercury* was equally enthusiastic about the poems:

'Since the days of Burns we believe that no provincial dialect has been honoured by becoming the vehicle of true poetry, in any degree approaching this, and we have every reason to hope, that Mr Barnes's simple lays will embalm the good old-fashioned language of Dorsetshire, and secure it a memorial as long as the Doric and Scotch shall be unforgotten.'

Like the *Chronicle*, the *Mercury* reviewer assumed the 'simplicity' of the poems and it was many years after their first publication that critics such as Gerard Manley Hopkins, Hardy and
Geoffrey Grigson first identified their metrical artfulness. The
Mercury, as was to be expected, differed from the *Chronicle* on
the social value of the poems, praising them for keeping alive
'the interest in the affairs of the poor' and for supplying to
farmers and landlords 'a more intimate acquaintance with their
(the poor's) feelings and habits and a more sincere sympathy
with their wants.'[16]

The poems received attention in some national journals as
well. *The Literary Gazette* concluded that the book must have
been produced by one of extensive scholarship, which presumably indicates that the reviewer was impressed by the Dissertation and Glossary even if he could not make much of the
poems.

The most extensive review in a national journal came in
Barnes's old favourite, *The Gentleman's Magazine*. The December
edition contained an article of fourteen pages which quoted
many extracts and no fewer than fifteen poems full length. The
unsigned article was given prominence by its placing at the front
of the journal, which had the effect of pronouncing the publication of the poems to be a major literary event, which was no
doubt the intention of the editor, Barnes's old friend Gough
Nicholls. The reviewer explained to the reader that he did not
know the poet personally but, Nicholls found himself bound to
add in honesty, that the poet had been a contributor to the
magazine for many years. This extremely perceptive review was
the first to note a significant element in Barnes's claim to be a
major poet, that the poems were entirely original in thought and
language:

'Poets like all other persons, must have their thoughts strongly affected
and acted on by the sympathies of their own times, and by the minds of
their contemporaries ... But we are bound in fairness to say that in Mr
Barnes's poems we can trace no footsteps of the submissive or sequa-
cious follower of any poetic school or model, but that of true nature and
passions. The poet's heart is at home – his scenery is all domestic – his
circle of description of home growth, confined to his own fields and
boundaries; and the little village scenes, the household cares, and

employments, the innocent pleasures, the gentle sorrows and joys, the rural pastimes, the business and amusements – he places before us, and throws into dramatic form, and invests with personal interest, are all drawn from the characters familiar to him.'[17]

But the sales of the poems were disappointingly slow in the spring and summer. *The Gentleman's Magazine* article appeared too late in the year to bolster the early sales. What Barnes needed in April and May was a patron, some friend at the court of literature, willing and able to push poetry in genteel society where reputations needed to be made. His publisher, John Russell Smith, wrote to him in May to complain that the poems are 'hardly known' in London and that he has sold very few copies. He advised that a little money might be spent on advertising.

Barnes's first and only excursion into literary society came with an invitation to a house party at Frampton House, the home of Richard Brinsley Sheridan, the grandson of the dramatist. The party was to include two of his three beautiful sisters, known locally as the 'three graces', in this case, Lady Dufferin and the Hon Mrs Caroline Norton. There were to be, in addition, the Dean of Westminster, two bishops, an archdeacon, and the editors of the *Royal Agricultural Journal* and the *Examiner*. At first, Barnes refused the invitation, on the ground that he was 'unaccustomed to society' but was subsequently persuaded. Julia, it seems, was not invited. Sheridan afterwards recollected that Mr Barnes had much impressed 'all the distinguished persons ... by the simplicity, varied knowledge, and information he imparted on so many subjects of interest'.

Caroline Norton was particularly struck with him. It was she who had so earnestly pleaded with her brother to invite the obscure Dorchester schoolmaster. Barnes, the worthy and piously-respectable young schoolmaster of Norman's House, was dazzled and gratified by the notice of this society woman. Caroline Norton, an early feminist, a poetess, and a nationally-controversial figure, was touched and secretly flattered by Barnes's evident admiration. Her career was a matter of public record. In 1827 she married the Hon George Norton, an indolent barrister who had turned out to have a violent temper and a dullness of intellect. Caroline had prevailed upon her friend, the then Home Secretary, Lord Melbourne, to find a job for George and he had indeed been awarded a metropolitan police magistracy. However, in 1836, Norton had brought an action against Melbourne for seducing his wife. The action was dismissed and the defence let it be known that they considered the whole thing to be a Tory plot to discredit Melbourne so that he might not become the Prime Minister to the new Queen. Thereafter, Norton and his wife lived apart but he constantly harassed her by denying her the right to the custody of her own children and even to her own income. He earned very little, whereas she was receiving £1,500 a year from the royalties on such ballads as *The Arab's Farewell to his Steed* and *Not Lost but Gone Before*. Eventually, Caroline's passionate writings in her own defence directly influenced new legislation which much improved the rights of married women. Caroline died in 1877, and in 1885, George Meredith fictionalised her life in *Diana of the Crossways*.

From the time of their meeting at Frampton House, Caroline Norton appointed herself Barnes's friend and patron. She set herself to promote his poems among her influential friends in London. The effect she had may be deduced from the change in the publisher's letters to Barnes. In August he wrote to say that he was quite sold out of the *Poems of Rural Verse* and would Barnes send fifty more copies. Caroline invited her protege to visit her in London, and he did so later in the month on the pretext of visiting his publisher. They visited Professor Wheatstone, who demonstrated the workings of his galvanic telegraph between Slough and London. Barnes was much excited by the exhibition and stored up as much of the information as he could to communicate to his pupils. After an early dinner at 6.30pm, Mrs Norton took him to the opera. He enjoyed the performance but was rather shocked that the social events continued into the sabbath day. In November, Caroline Norton wrote to say that she had discussed his work with the Rev John Mitford at the home of the poet, Rogers, and Mitford had spoken highly of the Dorset poems. Barnes was so taken with Mrs Norton's flattering attention that he addressed a sonnet to her:

TO THE HON MRS NORTON, THE POETESS, ON MEETING HER AT FRAMPTON HOUSE

When first I drew, with melting heart, alone,
  (O gifted vot'ry of the tuneful nine,)
  Entrancing melody from songs of thine,
Sweet echo'd words of one as yet unknown;
How much I wonder'd what might be the tone
  Of her true voice, as yet unansw'ring mine,
  And what the hue with which her eyes might shine,
And what the form in which her soul was shown

To sons of men. How busy fancy brought
  Before me lineaments of love and grace;
    But who can tell what joy was mine at last,

When I beheld the object of my thought,
  In bright reality before my face,
    And found the fairest of my dreams surpass'd.[18]

History does not record the comments of Mrs Barnes on this poem.

Caroline Norton not only attempted to promote the poems, she attempted to influence their form. In this respect she was one of the first to try to persuade Barnes to change his manner of writing. She wrote to him:

'I much wish you would put some of them into more Cockney English. Perhaps you would let me send a list of those which are most liked, and would easiest bear the transmuting power proposed to be applied to them. Then you would judge if we were right in our selection.'

Twenty years later Alexander Macmillan, the publisher, was communicating to him similar sentiments from a reader: 'What a pity Mr Barnes *will* write that dialect! I really cannot, even after much pains, get at the meaning, and the effort too often exhausts the interest.'[19] Despite this, local audiences were beginning to receive performances of the dialect poems with delight. In the winter of 1844, for instance, the Rev W. Henning read some of them at the Sherborne Literary Institution to an appreciative audience. Nevertheless, Caroline kept up the pressure. She wrote in November to ask 'Have you given up thoughts of rendering some of them (the poems) more easy for the common English reader?'

It would have seemed ungrateful for him to ignore the advice from kind friends. In 1846 appeared *Poems Partly of Rural Life in National English*, published again by John Russell Smith in London and George Simonds in Dorchester. The book contained sixty-four poems and cost five shillings. Unlike the dialect poems, which ran to four editions and three expansions, the poems in national English were never reprinted, a fact which bears upon the wisdom of Caroline Norton's enthusiasm for his poems in national English.

The English poems mark a clear falling off of poetic talent. Barnes's peculiar gifts are rarely evident in standard English. Of the national English poems only one, *Rustic Childhood* is truly effective and this poem, as expected, derives from his recollections of Blackmore:

> No city primness train'd our feet
> To strut in childhood through the street,
> But freedom let them loose to tread
> The yellow cowslip's downcast head;
> Or climb, above the twining hop
> And ivy, to the elm-tree's top;
> Where southern airs of blue-sky'd day
> Breath'd o'er the daisy and the may.
>   I knew you young, and love you now,
>   O shining grass, and shady bough.[20]

Most of these poems in national English might well have been written by any one of a number of minor Victorian poets. They employ no distinctive speaking voice as do the dialect poems. The themes remain constant but they lack the vigour, humour and bite of the originals. The poems in national English are, in truth, the conventional musings of a Victorian schoolmaster concerned to find favour with an audience of genteel readers. Mrs Norton was wrong. Though she was most helpful in attempting to publicise his poetry, she was no judge of its merits and, therefore, became a harmful influence upon it. Some years later Barnes published a second volume in National English but, like the first, it was not reprinted. Meanwhile the Dorset poems gradually attracted the genuine admiration of poets with a national reputation.

7
Jay A Pass'd; Dorchester
1847-1862

Until the rejection of his application for the headship of Hardye's Grammar School in 1847, William Barnes's life had been one of a steady progress from the impoverished state of his boyhood. He had prospered in his business, risen in his profession, established himself as a scholar and enjoyed a happy marriage blessed with clever children. His expectations of life were high when he entered into his new school at Hawkins's old house. He was already a clergyman and would soon be a graduate of Cambridge University. How should he fail to thrive? Nothing, at that time, could have prepared him for the series of blows that fate was about to deal him, for, in the next decade, he lost his partner, came close to bankruptcy, and learned daily to endure the contempt of many tradesmen in the spiteful little town. Years later he speculated in a poem on the loss of his happiness:

> Wer it when, woonce, I miss'd a call
> To rise, an' seem'd to have a vall?
> Or when my Jeäne to my hands left
> Her vew bright keys, a dolevul heft?
> Or when avore the door I stood,
> To watch a child a-gone vor good?
> Or where zome crowd did laugh aloud;
> Or when the leaves did spring, or die?
> When did my jaÿ all pass me by?[1]

The 'vall' referred to may be the defeat he suffered at the hands of the Feoffees of Hardye's; Jeane is, of course, Julia, who died in 1852; the child gone from home may be an anticipatory image of a parting to come. We cannot be quite sure whether the reference to the crowd laughing aloud indicates a particular event or whether it summarises the treatment he received at this time at the hands of his fellow townsmen.

Such behaviour must have seemed impossible when, at Michaelmas, in 1847, he moved with his wife, six children, cook, two maidservants, handyman and two or three ushers, to the imposing building of 40 South Street, Dorchester. It was just across the road from Norman House but much grander. Even so, from the moment in the spring, when Hawkins had accepted his revised offer of £700 to include carpets and fittings, Barnes and Julia had planned and effected major alterations to enlarge the property. There was an extensive garden running down to Back South Street, in which Barnes had constructed a new school-room. It was built of brick and the external walls were slated; it had an entrance of wooden steps from the rear. So soundly did Mr Lucas, Barnes's builder, do his work that the building lasted well into the twentieth century and was, finally demolished in October 1965. Beneath the schoolroom was a playroom, and Barnes ordered further alterations to the house itself to provide ample living accommodation for his family. All this work suggested high hopes for the future, and his optimism was justified when within a year, the school totalled 45 boys of whom no less than 28 were boarders. He could not have guessed that this would be the highest number that the school would ever boast.

His attention to the school's move was distracted by the need to keep up his terms of residence at St John's College. Regulations required a ten year's man to keep three terms in college, and he departed for Cambridge in May 1847, for a seven week course of study. Initially he enjoyed the experience. He shared the company of resident scholars for the first time in his life and fully exploited the resources of the College library, many of whose books were of a linguistic rather than a theological nature. He had been thrilled at the ceremony of the Queen's visit to Trinity College. He did not, however, feel that he could afford to spend a guinea on the great 'fete' (or public breakfast), nor did he buy a ticket for Jenny Lind's concert, which must have involved a considerable effort of self-denial in so musical a man.

The problem for a ten year's man, such as he, was to fit all the necessary tasks into the periods of residence. Barnes had completed his Latin and English sermons in his first term but had to wait until the autumn before he could arrange his required 'opponencies' (or debates in Latin) with other students. On

October 19, only eight days after his new school opened, he was back in Cambridge to debate the proposition that the Old Testament was not contrary to the New. Gradually it became apparent to him that the requirements of the degree for Bachelor of Divinity would necessitate far more than the three terms of residence that were formally prescribed. In all he completed seven terms of residence; in the spring and autumn of 1847, three times in 1848 and twice in 1850. On the 30 May 1847, on the fourth day of his first term, he had written to Julia to describe his feelings as 'truly happy ... as happy as the day is long', but, by the end of his course in 1850, the attendance at the College was a weary chore and he had no heart for it.

He had not anticipated that the completion of his degree would be such an interminable business, nor that it should be so detrimental to the interests of his school. So serious, indeed, was the effect that his absences from Dorchester were having, that he promised Julia at the end of 1848 that he would not return to Cambridge for the following year. While he was away the entire weight of school business was thrown upon Julia. It was she who ran the household, superintended the boys' personal welfare, attended to parents and solicited more scholars. Though she was more than competent at these tasks, Barnes had reason to fear for her fragile health. Now she was in early middle-age her workload was beginning to exhaust her; she was subject to fatigues, colds and minor ailments that worried him.

His absences also placed greater strain upon the academic staff. The senior usher, Isaac Hann, was given much more work to do and the studies of the schoolmaster undoubtedly tested the loyalty of him and his two juniors. Then again, the parents began to complain. A Mrs Williams suggested that she was not getting her money's worth with the schoolmaster away, then others took up the cry. It was all very well to write instructions to his staff daily from Cambridge, or grandly to order yet another half holiday for the boys, but parents had a right to expect that he should be attending to his business at the school.

Almost from the moment that he entered Hawkin's house, the fortunes of Barnes's school began to decline. The really profitable pupils were the boaders and their numbers dropped from 28 in 1848, to 18 in 1850 and 17 in 1851. No doubt there were factors other than his Cambridge absences involved, but they certainly made many a parent feel that his boy was not receiving the schoolmaster's full attention. Parents had then plenty of other local schools from which to choose, including Maskew's grammar school. Private schools were much more competitive since Barnes first started in Durngate Street. Peel's repeal of the Corn Laws was beginning to bite into agricultural prosperity; if there were more schools from which parents might choose, there were also fewer parents willing to pay the higher fees which Barnes now thought he could command. Of course, Julia could proudly extol her husband's academic eminence to doubtful parents and Barnes himself could inform his ushers, Hann and Brown, that his absences in Cambridge not only fitted him to be a better teacher but also, indirectly, benefitted them in the training they received. Both groups found such arguments rather hard to swallow.

It was fortuitous that the railway came to Dorchester in 1847, the very year when Barnes began his Cambridge visits. Not only could he travel to and from college within journeys of a single day but he was also within very swift postal contact with his family. A letter written on his fourth visit suggests that he liked to think of himself as Il Penseroso, the solitary student toiling for the truth in an antiquated setting:

St John's College
November 1st, 1848

My Dearest Julia,
I came up in exactly the way I marked out, but from the slipperiness of the rail I was late in London, and arrived at the Eastern Counties' station at the last minute.

Mr B. (my tutor) had found me a room and sent in a sack of coals and a bedmaker ready to receive me, and a porter met me at the lodge to show me the way to my abode. I am in that part of the college which the men call 'wilderness', one side of the first or oldest court.

I ascend to my room by a dismal dusty decayed staircase of dark oak, trodden by gownsmen of many generations. My room is large and lofty, and is partially lighted by a great window with stone mullions, but unluckily the fireplace is in the same wall as the window and therefore in a dark corner, so that I can hardly read in the luxurious attitude in which I indulge myself at home, with my feet on the hobs, or with my nose

resting over the grate. I guess the room might have been so built to give
the students a hint of the difference between light and heat.

I am making something of my time by reading. You might have found
me if you had come this morning with a huge folio (the works of an
ancient church father) before me. I wish to do as well as possible at my
examination, and can have from the library books that I should not and
could not buy . . .[2]

What is surprising about this letter is the revelation that
Barnes felt that he had to 'make something' of his time in Cambridge. His terms were by no means entirely taken up with study
for his degree. Nevertheless he committed himself to prodigious
reading programmes chiefly, it would seem, to support the
writing of his book *A Philological Grammar* which was to come
out in 1854. On January 25, 1850 for example, he had on loan from
the University library; David's *Modern Greek Grammar;* J.W. Pol,
Bohmusche Sprache; Ziegenbalg, *Grammatica Danubica;* End-
licker's *Chinesischen Grammatik;* Blazewicz's *Wallachian Sprache*
(Xylander); *El Arte del Bascuenze; Chaldee Grammar.*[3]

Only those who have attempted a part-time university degree
can understand with what expense of spirit and nervous energy
Barnes had attained it. His last visit to Cambridge was in
October 1850 when he had conferred upon him the degree of
Bachelor of Divinity. His only notebook entry on the matter
reads: 'At last, in 1850, at a more trying cost of time in residence
in Cambridge then even of money, I took my degree.' Even at the
last there had been a hitch. The dilatory College administration
had discovered, late in 1849, that he was now a lifeholder. Initially his fees had been waived but he had now a different
financial status and the recognition of this by the College for a
time threatened his entire registration. It seemed that he might
be required to pay high retrospective fees, or even that his
registration was invalid thus consigning thirteen year's work to
waste of effort. Eventually it was sorted out in his favour but, by
then, he had incurred further damage to his interests by protracted absence from Dorchester, and had grown tired of the
whole business.

Barnes took little from Cambridge other than a degree. He was
a scholar when first he went there. He seems to have made no
lifelong friendships or even useful acquaintances while there,

though it is characteristic of him that he was always elicited a warm greeting from the College servants. Nevertheless he had at last obtained the imprimatur of a scholar. In the New Year of 1851 he felt that he had arrived. He was a clergyman and a graduate, the principal of a successful (until recently) private school.

Remarkably, he had continued to write and publish books even whilst studying for his degree course. Another primer appeared in 1847, *The Outline of Geography and Ethnography for Youth*[4]. In 1849, the year in which he kept his promise to Julia not to return to Cambridge, his pent-up energies has resulted in no fewer than three books, one an Anglo-Saxon primer, another a piece of research into social history, and a third on political economy.

Barnes had pioneered the teaching of Anglo-Saxon in the schoolroom and his 78 page textbook entitled *Se Gefylsta (The Helper): An Anglo-Saxon Delectus* was written up from lesson notes. As usual with his primers, it had no great sale beyond his own school. In the Preface he expresses the hope that 'Anglo-Saxon may yet take its place, though it should be but a small one, in the English schoolroom if not on the desk of the grammar-school'. (His references to grammar schools, after the Hardye's incident, are almost always dismissive). His arguments for teaching Anglo-Saxon in school are rooted in the idea that the exercise is 'wit-sharpening', ie. that it promotes logical thinking. Educational research in our own day suggests that claims that such subjects as mathematics or classics improve the pupil's rationality in general matters are without foundation. Barnes's real reasons in promoting the subject were that he loved to learn and discuss old languages, and also that, in teaching Anglo-Saxon, he was given innumerable opportunities to point out to his scholars its close affinity with the Dorset dialect.

In the late 1840s and early 1850s his (temporary) affluence had enabled him to collect a library of old books and one of these was a small, calf-bound pocket-book that had served as the diary of John Richards of Warmwell, Dorset, between 1697 and 1702[5]. In 1849, Barnes used this book as material for a series of articles published in *The Poole & Dorset Herald* under the title 'Dorset-shire 150 Years Ago' and these articles were subsequently re-written for inclusion in John Russell Smith's *Retrospective*

Review in February and August, 1853. Richard's diary provides an informal, day-by-day record of his life as farmer and squire. He writes in note form and simply draws a line under each scribbled entry. It is part of Barnes's achievement as an historian that he was one of the first to understand the significance of such detailed material for scholars. In his articles he makes general deductions from Richard's unsystematic recording of his daily observations of sickness and medical treatment, sports such as horse-racing and cock-fighting, prices, wages, the condition of the poor and the conduct of the county election of 1701.

Barnes was not afraid to take on other historians, even the most eminent. Lord Macaulay's *History of England* had attained enormous success in 1848 when the first two volumes appeared. Macaulay, as a principal advocate of the Whig theory of history, had found it necessary to trace what he conceived of as the general improvement of the condition of the nation and, consequently, to denigrate its state in previous times. As an example he had pointed to the low remuneration of the clergy in the seventeenth century in contrast to the fatter stipends common under Victoria. This was a topic on which Barnes had peculiar knowledge. He was, after all, Stipendiary Curate of Whitcombe at £13 a year. He comments on Macaulay: 'It cannot be denied that there were low-paid clergy in the seventeenth century, as there are now. We know of one who, for some years, till within the last, held a curacy for £13 a year.'[6] Yet, as would be expected, Barnes's greatest objection to Macaulay's views is on the latter's smooth assumptions concerning the general improvement in language. Macaulay had written of his general notion of a seventeenth century farmer's conversation: 'his language and pronunciation was such as we would now expect to hear from the most ignorant of clowns. His oaths, coarse jests, and scurrilous terms of abuse, were uttered with the broadest of accents of the provinces.' Barnes comments: 'This is a charge which we should not think of hearing from a philologist or scholar, since we do not think the speaking of the dialect of a man's birthland is generally any token of coarseness or refinement.' The parents on whom he depended for his livelihood are unlikely to have agreed with him.[7]

Barnes contributed another series of articles to the *Poole &*

East Dorset Herald between April and May. It was entitled 'Humilis Domus' (which may be translated as 'The Humble Home') and concerned itself with the housing of the agricultural workers of the county. Barnes anticipates the plans for ideal cottages for manual workers which were exemplified at the Great Exhibition of 1851. His arguments combined moral and sanitary criticism. A 'foul house life', he argued, can be perpetuated for generations. Workers' cottages should be free from disease and should afford separate bedrooms for the sexes so as to ensure the moral decencies. He was probably thinking of the crowded hovels in Mill Street, Fordington, (Hardy's 'Mixen Lane') which had a population density comparable to Manchester.[8] He deplored the demolition of cottages by large landowners when there were so many 'houseless poor' in the county. He even anticipated the Welfare State by suggesting that, because the poor driven from demolished homes could not obtain poor-relief outside their own parish, rating and welfare should be provided at a county or even national level rather than by the parish.

Barnes's observations upon political economy derived from the same values that pervade his poetry. His ideal working man was an independent smallholder, like Uncle Charlie Rabbetts when he was free of debt and danger. Barnes's ideal economy was based upon an agricultural system in which each man has thirteen acres to feed his family. He was also concerned that such a life should not be all drudgery, and pleaded that the poor man should enjoy a few hours each evening 'free of hand toil' to 'purify and adorn' his family life. He argued that poor relief should be earned by work rather than distributed to those who do nothing, pointing out that he knew at least one parish church that needed its paths freshly gravelled. Above all he deplored those who championed emigration for the poor. For such people to leave the country in great numbers would, he argued, leave it in the hands of 'the gay and insolvent spendthrift.' His approbation is reserved for that fierce local loyalty from which true patriotism derides. 'For what is England', he demands, 'that she should be dear to me, but that she is the land that owns my county? Why should I love my county, but that it contains the village of my birth? Why should that village be hallowed in my mind, but that it holds the house of my childhood?'

After years of overwork and worry, Barnes felt that he owed his family a holiday. Accordingly, on 1 July 1851, early in the morning, a prospective passenger might have observed on the up-line platform at Dorchester station, a family party consisting of the Reverend William Barnes, B.D., Mrs Barnes, Miss Laura Barnes (aged 23) and Miss Julia (aged 18). They were to stay in London for four days in order to visit the Great Exhibition. The family took lodgings in Pimlico and sallied forth daily in pursuit of pleasure tempered by instruction. Barnes particularly admired Hiram Powers's statue of 'The Greek Slave' which was exhibited in the American pavilion under a canopy and on a bed of red plush. This exhibit was especially popular with visitors, its sub-erotic features being licensed for Victorians by its classical pretensions. Barnes bought and kept a relic of this chained and naked girl, and it remained in his bedroom till his death.[9]

The whole exhibition delighted the family and, for two days, they roamed the glass halls in Hyde Park, marvelling at the huge statue of Richard the Lionheart at the entrance, the myriads of inventions and contrivances, statuary, pottery, jewellery and handicrafts. Then, in the Great Hall, Barnes rounded an exhibit and came upon an old friend, a Blackmore man, the 20 stone Job Rose, who met them with a host of jokes and stories about his coming to London and how he had been treated by the 'natives'. Job's joke was that, when he tried to get into London cabs, he excused the problems caused by his girth by explaining that he himself was undersized for a Dorset man, thus proving the superiority of his native county to a London which could only breed whipper-snappers. From this account, Barnes composed a poem which proved to be a comic favourite with his audiences, *John Bloom in London*[10].

After their two day's at the Exhibition, Barnes and his ladies took trips to see the River Thames, London Bridge and also Greenwich where, in the Royal Naval College, they inspected the paintings of Sir James Thornhill, a Blackmore man. On the last day they visited the British Museum and left for Dorchester on the 3.30 train.

The visit to the Exhibition was remembered by Laura and Julia for many years afterwards as a high point in the family's happiness, and it acted as a sharp contrast with what was to follow.

His wife's health had long been a matter of concern to Barnes. In two decades she had borne seven children and managed four schools. Dorchester was an unhealthy place in the 40s and 50s, especially in the summers, and there had been frequent outbreaks of cholera, as well as lesser epidemics of measles and influenza. Schools were particularly vulnerable institutions and, though Barnes's academy seems to have escaped the cholera, one boy died there in 1850 of an unspecified ailment. In that same year, while Barnes was wearily travelling back and forth to Cambridge in the task of securing his degree, Julia had nursed her whole family through feverous attacks. Despite the help of a faithful (but inadequate) staff of Jane Hall, their cook, the two maids, Ann Guy and Martha Durman, and a daily handyman, the load upon Julia had become greater, especially as old Mrs Miles was ceasing to be very much help. It seemed inevitable that her own health would give way under the strain. Then, in the spring of 1852, her sister was suddenly widowed, and Julia departed for Nailsea to comfort her. When she returned to Dorchester at Easter it was obvious that she herself was not well. She complained of pains in the breast. By May 2 she had become bedridden. Barnes was quite distraught at this sudden decline in her health. He called in Doctor Cowdell who diagnosed what he chose to call an ulcer in the breast. Barnes demanded a second opinion but, most ominously, Sir Benjamin Brodie agreed with Cowdell in not recommending an operation.

The remaining weeks of the summer term were agony to the schoolmaster as hope alternated with despair and Julia's condition steadily worsened. He withdrew as curate of Whitcombe but was still obliged to fulfil long-standing commitments to take Sunday service and thus to lose precious hours with her. His mood rendered almost intolerable the gaiety and spirits of his youthful scholars for whom it was a summer like any other, replete with promises of cricket, bird's nesting, outings and dormitory parties. On 5 June, Barnes suddenly began to keep an Italian diary again, feeling, perhaps, the language to be more private and more suited to the expression of his concern. At last the final end-of-year party was over and Laura and Julia had somehow packed the boys' boxes and seen them go their whooping way home. Now he could concentrate on his tragedy. On

June 12 he presented his dying wife with a little gilded table for her birthday, but she could barely smile her thanks. Nurse Dent was with her all the time now, except when he sat by her, holding her hand. On 21 June 1852, came the moment of his greatest trial and he confided his thoughts to his English diary:

'Monday 21st. – Oh day of overwhelming woe! That which I greatly dreaded has come upon me. God has withdrawn from me his choicest worldly gift. Who can measure the greatness, the vastness of my loss? I am undone. Lord have mercy upon me. My dearest Julia left me at 11.30 in the morning.'[11]

The entries in his Italian diary for June 22nd and many days after is simply 'Giorno d'orrore'.

In July the school filled again with giggling rowdy boys few of whom, in all probability, gave more than a thought to the absence of Mrs Barnes. But they had need to. For now Miss Laura and Miss Julia had charge of them, inspected their boxes and their linen, and supervised them at meals, and the change was not a happy one. For Laura and Julia, now respectively 24 and 19 year's of age, the management of the school was an apprenticeship to drudgery. They hated it for, like their brothers and sisters, they had aspirations to higher callings. Laura was artistic and nourished the hope of studying painting abroad; Julia was the musical one with a voice that conjured universal admiration in Dorchester; Lucy fancied herself as a writer and was already at work on her first novel; Isabel was more absorbed with her appearance and clearly hoped for marriage when she was of age. Of the two boys, Barnes had always hoped that Willie would follow him to St John's and become ordained, while Egbert loved to make models of steam engines and was clearly destined to become an engineer. With so many children to feed, Barnes felt that he had to continue his school, if only to free his daughters from its service.

Old friends sustained him in his grief. Frederick Smith arranged madrigal evenings and also persuaded him and his family to join an excursion to Bindon Abbey. Mr Patch came in to play chess with him in the autumn evenings and Barnes himself began to develop an interest in art. As a boy he had loved to take up the pencil and paintbrush and now he rediscovered such delights. In later years, when he could no longer paint and draw, he took to collecting pictures, especially those by the sottish John Thorne, and he also delighted to practise picture framing and restoring. Yet these attempts at reviving his spirits were partially undermined by a new loss. Old Mrs Miles died on February 23 1853. After her funeral he confided to his daughters, 'I sink a step lower in sadness' and then withdrew to his study. A comparison of portraits charts his physical and mental decline over these years. The schoolmaster of John Thorne's painting is a vigorous man in the pride of his force and intellect; a photograph of the early 50s displays a withdrawn, white bearded man, portly in body and dressed with obvious carelessness in an old cassock. He had aged rapidly. It was at this time that he began to favour such sartorial eccentricities as the wearing of a biretta, which habit did not reassure prospective parents. Such are the unfairnesses of life that he was blamed for the fact that his wife was no longer present to superintend the welfare of his pupils.

Barnes had always been a scholar by nature but in his grief he now turned to his books as a solace and a refuge. He noted of those years that: 'I took in my sadness to constant work out of school as well as in it.' Increasingly, the lonely schoolmaster dulled his sorrow by absorbing himself in writing a book on philology, *The Philological Grammar*. In a way he had been researching it for many years; at Mere when he began to educate himself as a linguist, on holiday with the Miles family in Wales, as a student poring over an obscure grammar in the library of St John's College. Now had come the time to sift his extraordinary knowledge of languages so that he could identify the fundamental principles that underlay *all* language. Throughout the sad summer of 1852 he toiled at his manuscript and, exactly a year after Julia's death, at midsummer 1853, he sent it off to John Russell Smith. Only then did he permit himself a brief relaxation after months of gloom; he went off to the Isle of Wight with his elder girls where they spent the time by walking the esplanades and watching the launching of the gunboat *Princess Royal*. On his return, he had to wait till February 1854 to receive the proofs, and the first copy was in his hands by March 27th.

The Philological Grammar draws upon no less than 72 languages as sources. They include not only the classical and modern European languages familiar to the well-educated in Barnes's day, but also such exotic tongues as: Albanian, Bretonne,

Chippeway, Cree, Esthonian, Gaelic, Hawaii, Icelandic, Illyric, Kafir, Khoordish, Lapponic, Malay, Maori, Mongolian, Sanscrit, Tonga, Wallachian and Wendish-Servian. None of his philological writings gives greater evidence of his staggering linguistic powers. His daughter noted of him that 'He could acquire enough of a language in a week or two to enable him to read and write it with a dictionary.' As a padagogue, however, he made no claims to have a natural linguistic ability, but argued instead that he had discovered the fundamental structures of language, a knowledge of which would afford *the* method by which others could attain a linguistic prowess such as his own. The fact that his own children was each fluent in two or three languages was itself a demonstration of the correctness of his theories.

Despite its laborious scholarship, *The Philological Grammar* did not revolutionise language teaching in schools as its author intended, nor did it gain him much profit or reputation. He received the usual £5 plus a few copies from John Russell Smith but, as Lucy noted, 'the book found very little favour with the general reader', the critics having little to add to the verdict of one of them that the book was 'a most valuable monument to a well-read man's mental capacity.' Barnes had not wanted to be a monument but a force in philology. What else, however, could he have expected from the publication of a text in which grammar is reduced to enumeration by assigning numbers to each of the parts of speech and performing calculations upon them? Barnes's work in the field of philology anticipates in intention and, to some extent, method, writings in modern linguistics, but there were no prizes to be had for a Chomsky come-early. In some ways his book was an orthodox text, having sections in Orthography, Etymology, Syntax, Prosody and Rhyme, the last of these providing a magnificent encyclopaedia of verse forms which, incidentally, is profoundly helpful in the stylistic analysis of his own verse. In one way the book may be thought retrogressive. Lucy Baxter noted that 'The moment one opens the book one feels in a strange land.' This is due to the persistent Saxonising of the language. This is quite deliberate on Barnes's part. Not only does he defend the replacement of Latinisms by words originating in the Saxon tongue but the technical terms of the discourse are Saxonised. Thus vowels are referred to as 'breath-sounds' and consonants as 'clippings'.

In the summer of 1854, there was another outbreak of cholera in Dorchester. The worst area was Fordington, where the courageous evangelical, the Reverend Henry Moule, fought the moral and sanitary problems of Mill Lane day by day. Fortunately, Barnes's school was situated in a healthier district, half way up the hill, and once again his scholars escaped the dreaded infection. But there were the usual outbreaks of summer colds and fevers among the boys and the family, and Barnes himself became ill of some unspecified complaint.

In June he took his family on holiday to the Blackmore Vale. Here they explored the cool water-meadows and all the old haunts of the poet's boyhood. Yet on his return to Dorchester in July, Barnes became unwell again. His illness may have been psycho-somatic, for he dreaded another year of the grinding life of a schoolmaster with nothing to look forward to but mounting debts and loneliness. His complaint was initially diagnosed as gout and then toxaemia. As the months went by he experienced a stiffening of the joints of the hands. It was articular rheumatism. Even when he recovered his general health, his hands remained partly crippled and he lost for ever the capacity for that beautiful copperplate handwriting that had gained him a place in Mr Dashwood's office forty years before. From then on, his handwriting was large, ungainly, and frequently illegible.

His old friend, Charles Warne, invited him to London in the autumn. Barnes was unable to go, partly because of ill health and partly because he dare not leave the school. He went to town just after Christmas. Warne was an antiquarian and, in the New Year of 1855, he and Barnes visited the British Museum, the National Gallery, and attended a meeting of the Syro-Egyptian Society. Scholarly distractions were now Barnes's refuge from personal and professional gloom. He had little money for travelling far afield and so the local environment of Dorset, with all its antiquarian richness, became his playground.

In the summer he took his holidays again in Blackmore and visited Glanvilles Wooton and Stourton Caundle. He could not resist a visit across the border of Wiltshire to Chantry House where he was entertained kindly enough by the latest owner. Yet despite the friendly welcome and pleasant discussion his mind was absorbed by the sweet melancholy of old associations. It

was after this visit that he wrote the best known of all his poems,
My Orcha'd in Linden Lea:

> 'Ithin the woodlands, flow'ry gleäded,
>   By the woak tree's mossy moot,
> The sheenen grass-bleädes, timber-sheäded,
>   Now do quiver under voot;
> An' birds do whissle over head,
> An' water's bubblen in its bed,
> An' there vor me the apple tree
> Do leän down low in Linden Lea.
>
> When leaves that leätely wer a-springen
>   Now do feäde 'ithin the copse,
> An' païnted birds do hush their zingen
>   Up upon the timber's tops;
> An' brown-leav'd fruit's a-turnen red,
> In cloudless zunsheen, over head,
> Wi' fruit vor me, the apple tree
> Do leän down low in Linden Lea.
>
> Let other vo'k meäke money vaster
>   In the aïr o' dark-room'd towns,
> I don't dread a peevish meäster;
>   Though noo man do heed my frowns,
> I be free to goo abrode,
> Or teäke ageän my homeward road
> To where, vor me, the apple tree
> Do leän down low in Linden Lea.[12]

Wales

Meanwhile, Barnes's problems multiplied. Isaac Hann had
been his chief assistant or usher for twelve years and was concerned by the falling fortunes of the school. Hann foresaw the
school eventually foundering, and with it his employment. He
could also see that there was a new kind of market available
among tradesmen of the lower middle-class who wanted a more
practical education for their sons than was provided by Barnes's
or Hardye's. He gave in his notice at Michaelmas, 1855, and, on
30th November, he opened a rival school in Salisbury Terrace,
just a walk away from 40 South Street. Furthermore, he undercut
Barnes's fees. Barnes had not dared to lower his own charges for
it would have been interpreted as a mark of public failure. Hann
cannot be entirely blamed. He had long served out his apprentice-

ship and deserved to profit from his shrewd eye for new customers. Barnes's notes do not mention the incident but he wrote
quietly to Warne to observe that 'a late assistant of mine has
planted a desk here, on low terms, and done me, I think, much
harm.' While Barnes's school continued to decline, Hann's flourished. In five years he had four assistants working under him
and was obliged to remove to larger quarters in North Square.
Barnes's children were most indignant and, for years, preserved
the tale of Hann's perfidy.

Throughout this period, Barnes did his best to maintain ap-
pearances, playing his part in the museum, the musical life of the
town and the savings bank. Nothing absorbed him so much,
however, as his growing support for the newly-founded institutes for the provision of education to working men. These
self-improvement societies depended upon guest lecturers and
Barnes rarely refused a request to appear. In 1850 he had lectured
to the institute in Weymouth and, in 1851, with his old friends
Bingham and Moule, he helped to found the Dorchester Mutual
Improvement Society. In that year he gave the Dorchester
'mechanics' a series of lectures on philological and scientific
topics, beginning on 30th of November with an address on
'Light and Heat'. For the next twenty-five years he continued
this voluntary work, never accepting a penny in payment. He
travelled far afield from Dorchester, so that, by the 1860s he was
accepting invitations from towns in Hampshire, Wiltshire and
Somerset as well as his native county. There is still preserved in
the Dorset County Museum a testimonial presented to Barnes on
23rd February 1857 by the chairman, William Cole, and four
other members. It reads:

'This testimonial was presented with a silver pencil case, by the members
of the Dorchester Working Men's Mutual Improvement Society to the
Rev W. Barnes, B.D., as a small but grateful memento of the kind
assistance cheerfully rendered to their society, by the delivery of deeply
instructive lectures; and of the liveliest interest ever manifested in its
behalf. Anno Domini 1857.'

Lucy Baxter records that Cole spoke wonderfully well in making
the presentation. In reply to this completely unexpected tribute,
Barnes was moved to declare his feeling for them because 'he

himself had not been nursed in the lap of luxury, but was, like themselves, a working man.'[13]

It may be thought that his voluntary work for the mutual aid societies would have enhanced Barnes's prestige in the town. Such was not the case. Many middle-class people were opposed to societies of this kind on the grounds that education for the working classes was fuel for seditious talk. The memory of the 'Swing' riots of 1830 was by no means dead. Parents were especially critical. Was not the schoolmaster giving away free to working men the benefit of his knowledge for which they were expected to pay good money? Besides, a man who consorted nightly with mere mechanics and referred to himself as one of them was clearly unappreciative of the very social graces for which they were paying him. The schoolmaster should save his energy and keep his company for their sons.

Paradoxically, as Barnes's fame as a scholar increased, so the reputation of his school declined. That his scholarship was widely appreciated in all classes can be seen from the frequent requests he received to lecture all over the county both to working men and to antiquarian societies. Furthermore, he was sometimes consulted by a sixteen year old boy who, though not one of his pupils, could appreciate the master's knowledge of the classics. The young Thomas Hardy was an apprentice at Hicks's, the architect. He with young Horace Moule and Barnes's pupil, Thomas Hooper Tolbort, were an astonishingly bookish but light-hearted trio of young men to find in a small town. Florence Emily Hardy comments:

'At this time the Reverend William Barnes, the Dorset poet and philologist, was keeping school next door. Knowing him to be an authority upon grammar Hardy would often run in to ask Barnes to decide some knotty point in dispute between him and his fellow pupil. Hardy used to assert in later years that upon almost every occasion the verdict was given in his favour.'[14]

The publication of the second volume of the Dorset dialect poems extended a knowledge of his work to a yet wider audience, especially as the Reverend Nares Henning had for some years been giving public readings of them. In January 1856 he wrote to Barnes to express his admiration of the poems and to ask that he might be given a private reading of the poems by the author himself. Yet even such a well meaning man as Henning may have helped to have harmed Barnes's livelihood for he reminded the local community that the schoolmaster was a champion of the local dialect and, therefore, opposed the refined gentility that they wished for their sons.[15]

The second volume of dialect poems came out in 1858 and was entitled *Hwomely Rhymes*[16]. The book contains over a hundred new poems many of which celebrate the social life and natural beauty of the Blackmore scene. Among the new poems are *Blackmore Maidens*, which praises the beauty of the young girls of the Vale, *Bishop's Caundle* which recalls the feasting that terminated the Napoleonic Wars, and poems about local characters such as the contrasted pair of Gruffmoody Grim, the village misanthropist, and Gammony Gay, who radiates good will and elicits cheerfulness from all those he meets.

Much of the poetry explores the theme of lost love, old friendships and of joys passed. At the age of 58, Barnes had ceased to live emotionally in the world he actually inhabited. Here are no poems of Dorchester life, of town characters and gossip or of the trials of a teacher. His imagination was now elsewhere, either in the Blackmore of his youth, or else in meditations of all his life with Julia. One or two poems contrast the blissful innocence of his early days with the scepticism of modern times:

THE HAPPY DAYS WHEN I WER YOUNG

> In happy days when I wer young,
> An' had noo ho, an' laugh'd an' zung,
> The maïd wer merry by her cow,
> An' men wer merry wi' the plough;
> But never talk'd, at hwome or out
> O' doors, o' what's a-talk'd about
> By many now, — that to despise
> The laws o' God an' man is wise.[17]

By contrast, the Blackmore poems extol the values of old friends and familiar scenes. In them we glimpse pale faces of the wives long dead, such as that of Ellen Brine of Allenburn or that of the Squire's wife, to whom he dedicated a *Leady's Tower*

with illustrations of her life painted on the interior walls round a
spiral staircase:

> An' here ageän upon the wall,
> Where we do zee her last ov all,
> Her husband's head's a-hangen low,
> 'Ithin his hands in deepest woe.
> An' she, an angel ov his God,
> Do cheer his soul below the rod,
> A-liften up her han' to call
> His eyes to writen on the wall,
> As white as is her spotless robe,
> "Hast thou remembered my servant Job?"
>
> An' zoo the squier, in grief o' soul,
> Built up the Tower upon the knowl.[18]

He had begun to think of his own lost wife as an 'Angel',
perhaps influenced by Coventry Patmore's *The Angel in the
House* which had first appeared in 1854. No lines better convey
his profound sense of loss than a couplet from *The Leady's
Tower:*

> But still his ethly joys a-vled,
> His one true friend, his wife, is dead.

When Thomas Hardy's first wife died, in 1912, the elegiac
poems poured out of him, treating of his first meeting with her,
their life together and his subsequent loss. So it was for Barnes
sixty years before. A splendid poem entitled *The Bwoat* medi-
tates a first meeting with Julia transposed from Dorchester High
Street to the banks of the Stour. The names and locations are
unimportant; the true subject of the poem is the agitation of a
mind by the experience of love at first sight:

> Where cows did slowly seek the brink
> O' Stour, drough zunburnt grass, to drink;
> Wi' vishen float, that there did zink
>   An' rise, I zot as in a dream.
> The dazzlen zun did cast his light
> On hedge-row blossom, snowy white,
> Though nothen yet did come in zight,
>   A-stirren on the straÿen stream;

Till, out by sheädy rocks there show'd,
A bwoat along his foamy road,
Wi' thik feäir maïd at mill, a-row'd
    Wi' Jeäne behind her brother's oars.
An' steätely as a queen o' vo'k,
She zot wi' floaten scarlet cloak,
An' comen on, at ev'ry stroke,
    Between my withy-sheäded shores.

The broken stream did idly try
To show her sheäpe a-riden by,
The rushes brown-bloom'd stems did ply,
    As if they bow'd to her by will.
The rings o' water, wi' a sock,
Did break upon the mossy rock,
An' gi'e my beäten heart a shock,
    Above my float's up-leäpen quill.

Then, lik' a cloud below the skies,
A-drifted off, wi' less'nen size,
An' lost, she floated vrom my eyes,
    Where down below the stream did wind;
An' left the quiet weäves woonce mwore
To zink to rest, a sky-blue'd vloor,
Wi' all so still's the clote they bore,
    Aye, all but my own ruffled mind.[19]

The dream-like feeling of the opening wonderfully evokes the innocent unawareness of his boyhood. The disturbance of the water by the coming of the boat symbolises the swellings of a profound disturbance in his own mind occasioned by the first sight of her. His Julia was now lost and had floated from his eyes. There are, in the *Hwomely Rhymes*, a number of elegies addressed to Jeane or Mary, but none surpass the simple poem *The Wife A-Lost:*

Since I noo mwore do zee your feäce,
    Up steäirs or down below,
I'll zit me in the lwonesome pleäce,
    Where flat-bough'd beech do grow;
Below the beeches' bough, my love,
    Where you did never come,
An' I don't look to meet ye now,
    As I do look at hwome.

Since you noo mwore be at my zide,
  In walks in zummer het,
I'll goo alwone where mist do ride,
  Drough trees a-drippen wet;
Below the raïn-wet bough, my love,
  Where you did never come,
An' I don't grieve to miss ye now,
  As I do grieve at hwome.[20]

Just once in his life did William Barnes have the opportunity to
achieve national fame as a poet. In October 1858 his friend
Charles Tennant, having been enthused by the latest volume of
poetry, wrote to invite Barnes to stay with him in London and
also to suggest that he give a 'Society' reading of his poems.
Tennant had received assurance of support from Caroline
Norton and the Duchess of Sutherland. A reading was planned
for May 1859 but had to be cancelled because of an illness in the
Duchess's home at Stafford House, where it was to be held. A
further attempt to hold the reading in June had to be cancelled
because of the dissolution of parliament which, wrote Tennant,
had 'driven pastoral poetry out of people's heads.' It had been
whispered that Sidney Herbert, then Secretary for War, would
be present, and even the Queen herself had been discussed as
one of those who would attend. In the event, the reading never
took place and the greater part of 'Society' remained unaware of
the existence of William Barnes throughout his life.

Yet Barnes did give a triumphant reading of his poems, not to
London salons but in the Town Hall in Dorchester. Tennant had
advised him to try out his poems on a Dorset audience and, on
5th October 1858, the hall was packed to hear the well-loved
poems read by the author himself. No doubt it was a biased
audience. Many of those present were members of the town's
working men's institute and, therefore, were devoted admirers
of Barnes. But local pride does not entirely explain what followed:

It was an evening to be remembered. The hall was thronged almost to
suffocation with rich and poor, and seldom has an audience been more
excited by various emotions. At one moment the whole mass of people
would be breathless with interest at such descriptive poems as "Jeane's
Wedden-day in Mornen," "Grammer's shoes;" the next, the women
would be sobbing audibly over "Meary Ann's Chile," or "My Love's

Guardian Angel;" then *hey presto!* sorrow would flee away, and the multitude of faces relax into smiles, with now and then a burst of hearty laughter, at "What Dick and I done," or "A bit o' Sly Courten'." It seemed to one of the poet's children that the crowd of human beings was a magic harp on which he played, bringing forth at his will the emotion he chose.[21]

The rural audience had never heard the like of it. Here was their own familiar tongue returned to them as literature; here were their lives presented as art. Barnes that night was pre-eminently a 'man speaking to men' – in concordance with Wordsworth's definition of a poet. At that moment, the Dorset poems were revealed as works which validated the rural experience of the audience. The occasion was a watershed in Barnes's life as a poet. Hitherto he had written for a genteel public, many of them removed from the language in which he wrote. After 1858 he became a popular poet in his own county, the voice of the people themselves. For many years after, he received countless invitations to read to working men's institutes throughout the county and beyond and his audience often walked many miles to hear him.

For all that his financial position became monthly more precarious. In 1857 his school still boasted a cricket team good enough to beat Hardye's but, by the following year, it could not muster a full team. Illness, withdrawals, and the rivalry of others such as Hann, had seriously undermined his establishment. He tried to make a little extra money by acting as a relief to a number of local clergymen but this produced no more than about £65 a year. A dreadful moment came in July 1859, when, on the resumption of the school term, Laura went into the schoolroom to find her father sitting alone at his desk with not a single pupil. He remarked gravely: 'You see, I am at my post.' He went on sitting there for two hours until a few boys eventually came in. The experience alarmed him deeply for, sitting at the empty desks he could spy in his mind's eye, penury, misery and perhaps, even, destitution. He had not forgotten the selling up of Uncle Charlie Rabbetts in the Vale. At this time he felt the growing contempt of a number of local tradesmen, some of whom he had dealt with for years. He had always loathed their pecuniary attitude and once said to his children: 'If I ever become rich

I shall hold a bag of gold in front of me as I walk abroad, so that
they may bow to it and not to me.' On receiving yet more letters
announcing the withdrawal of pupils, he complained, with considerable foresight, 'What a mockery is life! They praise me and
take away my bread. They might be putting up a statue to me
when I am dead, while all I want now is to live. I ask for bread
and they give me a stone.'

The only solution to the financial problems brought about by
the impending failure of his school was that of starting again and
finding another post, no easy thing for a man in his late fifties.
He applied for the post of Principal of the Diocesan Training
College at Winchester but was offered only the Vice-Principal-
ship at £100 a year, a sum inadequate to support the needs of his
family. He was subsequently rejected for the post of Chaplain to
Dorchester Asylum and even for the chaplaincy at Forston
Asylum.

Meanwhile he continued with his few scholars and his evening audiences of working men. He delivered to the latter some
lectures on the Ancient Britons and published the material in a
little book, in 1858, entitled *Notes on Ancient Britain and the
Britons*. He clearly felt qualified to teach the subject on the basis
of his knowledge of Welsh, which he seems to have regarded as
the original speech of the Britons. An epigraph on, the title page,
declares:

> To study tribes without their speech
> Is to grope for what our sight should teach.

Barnes told his audience of mechanics of the life of the Britons,
their clothes, chariots, food, burials, tattooing, houses and
roads. He would quote the evidence of archaeology and also the
writings of such authors as Caesar and Strabo. Frequently he
would tell a homely little tale to illustrate a point, such as his
account of a Welsh walking tour in 1856, which was supposed to
prove the proud independence of the Welsh (or British) nation.

Apparently, he had been walking in the Vales of the Neath and
Taff with a friend in hot weather, and they had gone into an inn
and ordered ginger beer (Barnes was an officer of the temperance
movement). The ginger beer was not enough to slake their thirst
and they had ordered glasses of water in addition. Their mistake

had been to offer to pay for the water. The landlady, who was a true Welshwoman (or Briton), knew the obligations expected of a host and refused to accept payment. Furthermore she stalked out and refused to speak to them any more. Barnes was delighted with her sturdy British contempt for him, and so, no doubt, were his students.

At last, in 1859, came the first signs of hope in his situation. In the summer, the whole family had moved to the lovely thatched Rectory of Winterborne Came, so that Barnes might act as a locum for the Reverend Lionel Damer whilst he was away. They loved the house and garden and returned to South Street with a longing to go back to Came. Astonishingly, this now seemed possible. Captain Damer, who owned the living of the parish, had been a private pupil of Barnes's. On an evening when he had invited his old master to dinner, Damer quietly informed him that he did not think that his cousin would remain as the Rector of Came for very much longer and that, when there was a vacancy, he would offer it to Barnes. The promise was of para-dise, a prospect which would, at a stroke, solve Barnes's worldly problems. He would not allow himself to dwell upon it too much, however. Barnes had more certain knowledge of the remarkable progress of his family. By delving into what savings he had left, he had launched his sons and daughters on the world. In January 1860 Willie had gone up to St John's at a cost of £50 in fees. On the 18th February, Egbert had been apprenticed to Mr Gooch at the railway workshops, Swindon, at a premium of £150. Julia had left home a little earlier for Germany, where she was to be trained as a singer. She was soon writing home to declare excitedly that she had been provided with a tutor by no less a person than the Princess Frederick Wilhelm. Apparently the princess had heard of her through the English Chaplain who knew Mr Barnes's writings on philology. Lucy, meanwhile, had completed her first novel, and planned to study art in Italy.

Of his children, only Laura would soon be left at home. She was a rather severe young woman, who shared her father's strong artistic and religious impulses. Though she later studied art at South Kensington and Florence, it seems that she had experienced some form of vocational commitment to helping her father's work, and to devoting herself to such good causes as the

Mission to Deep Sea Fishermen. She was especially interested in the welfare of the seamen of Labrador. By contrast, Isabel was pretty and rather superficial. Her vocation was for marriage. She had become engaged to the Reverend Joseph Shaw and, on 21 June 1860, they were married, and soon departed for his parish in the Lake District.

By the 1850s, Barnes's talents had been noticed by some beyond Dorchester. The local tradesmen may have shunned him but the Chevalier de Chatelaine called upon him with the request that he should be allowed to publish a selection of the Dorset poems in his *Beautés de la Langue Anglaise*. An even more distinguished Frenchman, Prince Lucien Bonaparte, called twice in 1859 to persuade Barnes to translate *The Song of Solomon* into the Dorset dialect. Proof of Barnes's talents as a schoolmaster was at last made manifest by the success of his pupil, Thomas Hooper Tolbort, who came first in languages and second in English, in the Oxford University public examination list for all England.

Yet the only improvement to Barnes's financial status was made not by himself but by a young solicitor named Frederick Cozens. He had long admired Barnes and took it upon himself to collect signatures from local notables in support of the inclusion of Barnes's name in the Civil List, as a poet of outstanding merit.

One topic that was especially frowned upon as a topic for working men's institutes was that of political economy, yet Barnes, at the height of his financial crisis, persisted in lecturing on economics to his manual workers. The result was a book entitled *Views of Labour & Gold* that came out in 1859. Knowledge of such texts as William Cobbett's *Cottage Economy* (1822) and John Stuart Mill's *Principles of Political Economy* (1848) had permeated the consciousness of many an artisan, but Barnes was determined to give them something different if just as controversial.

Labour & Gold is an idiosyncratic and rambling text-book of economics in which the author's approach is unashamedly linguistic. He seems to think that, if only he can give a clear *definition* of an economic concept, all related problems are solved. The opening of the book attempts to be systematic but the latter part is disconnected. The language is distinctly·Saxon.

Barnes's notion of value is based on what he calls 'lifegear', which is defined as 'that material in food or goods which we need to sustain life.' 'Lifegear' may be stored in the form of money but Barnes seems to disapprove of this custom. In Tonga, he pointed out to this pupils, a chieftain had complained of the introduction of money that, though it was useful because it could be carried about easily, it was harmful because it enabled a rich man to store his wealth. Apparently, in Tonga, the acquisition of wealth had hitherto been a matter for general rejoicing, because the only form of wealth known previous to money was food. As food was a perishable commodity, it had to be consumed immediately in tribal feasting. Money, on the other hand, encouraged hoarding and, therefore, selfishness.

Labour & Gold, unlike the philological books, takes its impulse from eccentricity rather than scholarship. For this reason, a systematic examination of Barnes's arguments on such topics as 'Capital' and 'Barter & Money' is nothing like so rewarding as savouring his digressions. He tells tales of the inventor, Erfinder, who devised a machine for pulling teeth but could not profit from it. In this book Barnes allows himself to parade some of his own prejudices, such as his belief that the entire American nation suffered from both avarice and indigestion. Apparently, ran Barnes's argument, Americans so worshipped Mammon that they gobbled their food as fast as possible in order to return to money-making – hence their indigestion. The language of the book is, at times, shot through with an oddity which derives from facetiousness. No doubt his scholars smiled at the examples he chose in order to illustrate the case against the scarceity theory of value: 'There is in England less weasel flesh than beef, and less badger quarters than quarters of mutton, and yet the commercial value of weasel flesh and badger joints is less than that of beef or mutton.' Few of his parents would have smiled to hear his analysis of the capitalist process in homely farm-yard terms: 'The kindness which is done by capital when it affords employment to people from whom, by monopoly, it has taken their little businesses, is such as one might do to a cock by adorning his head with a plume made of feathers pulled out of his own tail.' 'Mr Barnes', wrote Octavius Pickard Cambridge in his obituary, 'is severe upon capital.'[22] The only community of interest between master and man that Barnes can trace in this book takes its origin in Christian kindness.

Still there was no news from Damer. Isabel's departure in June 1860, had brought Barnes some slight financial relief but his affairs were still parlous. He received some relief, as well as hope, when a letter arrived containing an order for £30 as an earnest of Her Majesty's favour, to indicate that his name was still under consideration for the Civil List. Nevertheless, his affairs were so desperate at the time that he had to refuse an invitation to visit Warne in London pleading that it was an 'unprosperous time'. Friends tried to put a little money in his way. Tennant had introduced him to David Masson, the editor of *MacMillan's Magazine,* who now wrote offering to pay him £1 a page for articles. The first of these, 'Beauty & Art' appeared in the issue for May 1861.

Barnes's life at this time was full of contradictions, despair and hope, rumours, readings, apathy and intense work. In the spring of 1861 came a letter with dreadful news; Isabel had learned that her young husband of nine months was dying of tuberculosis. Laura departed quickly for the Lake District to help in the sick room. Then, one day in April, when only Lucy was at home, she was interrupted, while arranging some primroses in a bowl, by two gentlemen who said they had called to congratulate her father. They had read in *The Daily Telegraph* that he had been awarded a Civil List pension of £70 a year. (Barnes was well aware that, wonderful news though this was, it did not relieve his immediate circumstances because payment did not start till the following year.) Almost immediately following this piece of intelligence came the news that his son-in-law, Joseph Shaw, had died.

In the midst of such lurching fortunes, Barnes had always his books in which to bury himself. He was now working on the manuscript of the oddest of them all. It came out in 1861[23] and was called *Tiw; or a View of Roots and Stems of the English as a Teutonic Tongue.* The book takes its name 'Tiw' from the god after whom the teutonic race is named. Each page presents a list of consonantal patterns, with interpolated asterisks that may be replaced by vowels. Barnes attempts to demonstrate here that such consonant formations, or 'roots', denote sets of related meanings. For example, the root B*ng signifies the notion 'to set up, or make up together, as in a store; in a bunch or mass; in a building.' From such roots, many 'stems' may be formed by varying the terminal consonants (or 'clippings'). Thus *one* of the stems from B*ng is B*nc from which we may derive such words as 'bank', bench, bunch and bunker, all of which suggestion the heaping up and enclosing of money, wood and earth. In *Tiw* Barnes traces hundreds of such stems to what he believed to be their 52 basic roots.

Barnes wrote long before the production of the *Oxford English Dictionary* which traced the origin of words 'On Historical Principles.' Willis D. Jacobs has rightly argued that the wonder is not that Barnes was sometimes wrong in his etymology but that he was so frequently right.[24] *Tiw* remains as the most extreme expression of Barnes's teutonising and also of his interest in the onomatopoeic theory of language, but the book is now of more interest to poets rather than scholars. One young poet read the book soon after it came out and at once began to make lists of roots and stems. Gerard Manley Hopkins was fascinated by the way in which words of similar sound seemed to share a community of meanings. While at Balliol he recorded such lists in his notebook: 'Grind, gride, gird, grit, groat, grate, geet ... Original meaning to strike, rub, particularly together ... etc.'[25]

In the New Year of 1862 Barnes departed on his now familiar round of poetry readings to the institutes at Mere, Shaftesbury and Bridport. When he got back, on 30th January, the event occurred for which the family had hoped and prayed for years. Colonel Damer wrote to offer him the living of Winterborne Came. Barnes accepted with joy and prepared to wind down the school. For the first time for years there was general joy in the household. Not only would the family be housed free for life but the living carried a stipend of £200 per annum. Barnes had no doubts. After 39 years as a schoolmaster he prepared to change his profession to that of country priest. Then, at the last moment, came an ironic twist of fortune. The last boys were packing their trunks to leave on 20th June when *The Times* announced that Thomas Hooper Tolbort, Barnes's pupil, had come top in the entire country in the examinations for the Indian Civil Service. A pupil from an obscure private school had beaten the products of illustrious public and grammar schools in all England. Barnes was at once deluged with applications from parents to tutor

their sons but he turned them down, pointing out that 'it took
two to do it.' Nevertheless, the event finally vindicated him as a
schoolmaster of extraordinary ability, whose scholarship, particularly in the language of the sub-continent, was as sound as it
was deep.

On 30th July 1862, the Reverend Lionel Damer called at South
Street to deliver the keys to the Rectory. The family moved out in
August. The carts were laden with 140 feet of bookshelving and
the little table that Barnes had given Julia on her last birthday.
But the scientific apparatus and all the impedimenta of the classroom was left behind to go to the sales. It fetched practically
nothing.

8

The Dorset Sage, Winterborne Came
1862-1886

On the morning of September 8th, 1862, an open carriage climbed
slowly up 'Tophill' on the Island of Portland, turned the hairpin
bend about half way up, and came to a rest on a grassy platform
overlooking Weymouth Bay. Two men alighted to survey the
autumnal scene. Looking north they could see all along the Chesil
and out across Lyme Bay. But the bearded clergyman, speaking
fluent French, pointed inland, over Portland Harbour with its naval
craft, and the pleasure waters of Weymouth Bay. Beyond, he told
his guest, was the Ridgeway and Dorchester, while fifteen miles to
the north lay Blackmore, where he had been born. The speaker was
William Barnes, until the previous month the principal of a failed
boys school in Dorchester. His guest was His Highness Prince
Lucien Bonaparte, cousin to the Emperor of France.[1]

Local people were not especially surprised to read brief reports
of the visits in the local papers. They now understood that Mr
Barnes was a great scholar whose books were reviewed in the
London press. The French prince, too, it seemed, was an authority on dialect and was eager to have the Gospels translated into
the speech of Dorset, Somerset and Wiltshire. It was only natural
that he should consult Mr Barnes upon such matters, for among
scholars differences of rank and fortune meant less than to those
who listened to the strains of the Morganblatter Waltz on Weymouth promenade, or who prodded cows with a stick at Dorchester market. The local newspapers confirmed the scholarly
nature of the meeting. The two men, it was reported, conversed
'on philosophical topics chiefly' on the journey from Weymouth
to Portland and had 'fraternized in various tongues, speaking
French, Italian, Welsh and Basque.' Having enjoyed views from
Portland, they had realighted, descended the hill, and eaten
lunch at the Breakwater Hotel.

The visit had taken place barely a month after Barnes had quit his school to become Rector of Came. The change in his life greatly stimulated his energies as a scholar. Hitherto his poetry-writing and philological research had had to be squeezed into a life of domestic routine and pedagogic drudgery, now he was free to read, write and lecture as he liked. Through his lectures to the working mens' institutes and through his dialect poetry he now had a circle of admirers in his own county. He also had the notice of a discriminating circle of scholars and critics beyond. One such, the Chevalier le Chatelaine, had eulogised him in the most extravagant of terms:

> *Au Révérend William Barnes*
> Dans le langue de Dorsetshire
> Avec un gout exquis, avec un art divin,
> Un style qui chacun admire,
> Vous nous avez rendu le naif et le fin
> Qui nous captive dans Shakespeare . . .[2]

While looking at the view with his French guest in the autumnal sunshine, Barnes felt that still his life held promise and that his great talents might achieve recognition. Spurred on by the opportunities of his new life he turned again to his studies and, in the next twenty years, wrote seven books, on grammar, poetry, history and logic. He had become a sage.

Yet, despite his scholarly interests, he laboured wholeheartedly at the work of a country parson. His piety and goodness were at once recognised by the humblest of his flock and in his sweetness of manner he resembled that other parson-poet, George Herbert of Bemerton. The Victorian age produced a number of scholars and poets who passed their days as rectors of obscure country livings. Some, such as the Reverend Sidney Godolphin Osborne, contributed to the cause of national reform through the columns of *The Times*. There were parson poets, such as Charles Tennyson Turner, parson diarists, such as Francis Kilvert, and parson naturalists, such as Octavius Pickard Cambridge, who had been a boy in Barnes's school and lived to become an international authority on arachnology.[3] As a philologist, Barnes was as great a scholar as any of his fellow clerics but, in the impression he made as a priest, is more to be compared with John Keble, whose personal integrity so impressed those who met him that more than one came away from such a meeting a changed man. Barnes's scholarship never extended to theology but he was on terms of simple Christian affection with the cottagers of his parish whom he visited once a fortnight for many years. His greatest influence as a priest was not in what he said but in what he was.

Barnes moved into the Rectory with Laura and Isabel in August 1862, and he was formally inducted as Rector of Winterborne Came in a service at Salisbury Cathedral on the 1st November. Laura Barnes, who lived with her father for the next twenty-four years, described the new home they had come to:

> The Rectory of Came is a cosy little nest – a thatched cottage with wide eaves and wider verandah, on whose rustic pillars, roses, clematis and honeysuckle entwine. It has a flowery lawn in front, and a sheltering veil of trees at the side. The poet's study was a room on the upper floor, which overlooked the sunny fruit garden, and here he could watch the blossoms expanding and falling from his apple and apricot trees, and see the breezes waving his feathery-headed asparagus.
>
> And how he enjoyed his garden and tended his shrubs! Sometimes he took a fancy to mow his own lawn, in memory of early days at Mere, but the use of a little mowing machine, the invention of later times, useful though it was, never gave him the same feeling as did the scythe of his earlier days, making its graceful curves.[4]

A more suitable dwelling for a country clergyman and poet would be difficult to imagine. Lucy Baxter has recorded that, for many years, her father's favourite dreaming place was at a certain corner of the lawn 'wherein in May a red hawthorn tree and a flowering laburnum mingled their shades on the grass' and where 'nestling near was a white rose, which had been trans-planted from the old home in town, in loving memory of her whose hands had tended it there, and whose pale face its blos-soms had dressed for her last sleep.'

The annual stipend for the parish was £200 a year with the Rectory provided for the incumbent. The amount was about £80 less than the national average and it was well for Barnes that he had in addition his Civil List pension of £70. Despite his relatively low income, he at once went to work. He recruited his two daughters as unpaid 'curates' and, with their help, devised a system of parish visiting. The entire parish was divided into four areas so that, with systematic visiting and long walking by the parson and his daughters, each parishioner was called upon regularly. The area took in Came House with its park and row of servant's houses, the tiny thatched hamlet of Whitcombe, the Tudor manor house with its estate, and many an outlying cottage. Apart from Came and Whitcombe there was also a third church, that at Farringdon, but it was, however, only a ruined arch in a field. Nevertheless, Barnes visited it at least once a year; he said that he went elsewhere to preach but that he went to Farringdon to pray. Education was not neglected by the one-time schoolmaster. There was a parish school run for many years by a Miss Croft, and Barnes visited it almost daily to teach, preach or merely greet the children. Then there was the Sunday school and night-classes for adults, which took place in the Rectory one evening a week.

Much of Barnes's life from now on was spent in walking the parish. He never allowed the weather to deter him from visiting and argued that a bit of cold and wet never hurt anyone. When it rained he would cover his head with a piece of sacking.

His daughters also became great walkers, although they must have remonstrated with Barnes that he was overtaxing his strength in walking up to fifteen miles a day in his late seventies.[5] Such a life enabled Barnes to cultivate his taste for eccentric clothing. He had now no parents to fear with their disapproving looks and he could wear his cloak and his Basque cap or perhaps his Turkish fez whenever he liked.

Thus began a long life of productive, peaceful regularity with a routine that hardly varied from year to year:

After breakfast he took a stroll round his garden, noting this and that blossom in its growth, then he gathered up the letters which had strewn his breakfast table, and proceeded to answer them. General correspondence was always more or less irksome to him, and so to get the thought of it off his mind he answered his letters as soon as he received them. These written, he would come down and place them in the green letter box under the verandah, which the postman cleared every evening, and with a sigh of relief would start off to visit his poor. The afternoon was spent in his study and in the evening he rested in his arm-chair in the drawing room, enjoying the music his daughters made for him.

From January 7th 1864 to the 3rd July 1865, Barnes kept a little diary whose brief entries help to fill out the details of his daily life. It opens with a list of accounts which record the fees he commanded as a preacher in neighbouring parishes: the usual payment was a guinea. Most of the entries record his daily round: gardening, reading, visiting the sick, writing sermons and visiting institutes to reach or teach. He still could not restrain the urge to educate others, despite the chastening experience of his school's decline. On 24th February the entries appear in Italian and continue so to the end. Many of them conclude with the name of his dead wife, 'Giulia', so that she was the last thought with him every day.

Barnes was now the paterfamilias of six children and a growing number of grandchildren. A phrenological sketch of his character made by a certain Edward Preston Mead describes him as:

'of rather warm and amative feelings and a thoroughly family and domestic man-strong in paternal love and in all domestic attachment. He is fond of home and country and all his warmest affections concentrate round the domestic hearth. The dearest spot to him is the Englishman's fireside, to him there is in reality, 'No place like Home.' He is adhesive to an almost diseased degree . . .'

Of his daughters, Laura and Isabel were still at home but both Julia and Lucy were married to Englishmen in Florence. The former had married a dental surgeon, Charles William Dunn, at Came in 1863, while the latter married Samuel Thomas Baxter in 1868. Between them the Dunns and the Baxters provided Barnes with eight 'Italian' grandchildren so that in the 1870's and 1880's there were frequent young visitors to Came in the summertime. Barnes was occasionally asked to make a return visit. In August 1870, for example, Lucy wrote to promise her father 'classical and antiquarian temptations' if he came to Florence. She anticipated his objections on the ground of cost by observing that 'If you would only let to some London clergyman in want of a holiday house and garden, he would not want payment for the light duties I am quite sure.' But not even the decoy of altruism could lure Barnes from his parish.

Egbert, the youngest of Barnes children, married Jane Creasy and presented his father with three more grandchildren. Unfortunately, Egbert's life as an engineer in the Swindon railway workshops was injurious to his health and he died in 1877.

By contrast, Barnes's elder son, William Miles, became his helpmate for the whole of his later life. Willie had followed his father as a student at St John's College, Cambridge. He may not have been very successful as a scholar for there is evidence of some sort of 'breakdown' before he was able to satisfy his examiners. He took his degree in 1863. He applied for a clerical post in Jamaica but was rejected and so was obliged to become a tutor in Ireland in the household of the splendidly-named McGillicuddy of the Reeks. Willie subsequently served as a curate in Tincleton, near Dorchester, and then, to his father's great delight, was appointed Rector to the parish of Winterborne Monkton, which adjoined that of Came. For the rest of Barnes's life he was able to count upon the support, help and companionship of his own son, who lived in the next parish. Willie was willing to take services and other duties so that Barnes was able to go on his lecture tours. In 1867, Willie married Emily Le Cocq of Guernsey and, over the next few years, there appeared two granddaughters and four grandsons for Barnes in the Rectory at Monkton.

Many of the entries in Barnes's journals during the 1860's and 1870's record that he has been lecturing or reading in another town, usually at an institute. The first months of September and October, when he entered into his new life, provided him with a promise of a wider scope for his talents than was ever allowed him in the old South Street days:

Sept 7th 1862 Prince Ll Bonaparte came with a set of his Highness's verses.
Sept 8th I went to Weymouth with him.
Oct 3rd Captain Damer signed my presentations.
Oct 14th I gave a lecture at Frome Somerset.
Nov 3 Reading at Sherborne
Nov 4 Salisbury for Institution
Nov 6 Lecture, Devizes, 'The Western English Dialect.'

Rarely now did he lecture upon scientific matters. It seems likely that the Darwinian controversy of 1859 had made him increasingly doubtful of the effect of scientific education because of its possible challenge to the claims of Christian belief. In later life, Barnes met Bishop Wilberforce of Oxford on several occasions and this was that same 'Soapy Sam' who had debated Darwinism with Huxley at the historic forums of the British Association for the Advancement of Science that had met at Oxford in 1860. It seems, however, that whenever Barnes met with him, the poet kept the topic of conversation away from anything controversial, and restricted their talk to antiquarian matters.[6]

It has been calculated that Barnes gave at least 178 lectures to working mens' institutes throughout Dorset, Hampshire, Wiltshire and Somerset.[7] After the publication of his third collection of dialect poems in 1863, he was in great demand as a lecturer upon the speech of the western counties and, naturally, he would illustrate his remarks by reading from the poems. As might be expected, the novelty of these occasions wore off more quickly in his own locality where they came to be taken for granted. In 1864 he attracted an audience of 900 at the Bristol YMCA, and even in 1868, over 230 people crowded the 'penny-reading' at Somerton Village Hall, with more left outside. At Weymouth, however, on his home ground, he had a 'cruelly disappointing evening' in 1869, with a poor response from the few who turned up, and on November 26, 1869, in Dorchester, the local newspaper explained the poor audience he attracted by declaring that his potential listeners 'were drawn off by a lecture at the National Schoolroom nearby.'[8] Clearly, his novelty value had worn off. This is further shown by his humble role in the 'Grand Soiree and Conversazione' given on December 19, 1867, to mark the opening of the new Corn Exchange in Dorchester. In a strictly-timed programme of events which included magical experiments, demonstrations of electric bells and fire-alarms, gas lamp improvements and harp solos, Barnes was allowed only ten minutes for the reading of his Dorset poems. No doubt the sight of this bearded old man reading verses from the long past must have seemed sadly anachronistic to an audience seeking the thrills of incandescent technology.

Two publications in the early 1860's supported Barnes's claim to be regarded as an expert speaker upon the dialects of the western counties. In 1863, the Philological Society published Barnes's first edition of *A Grammar and Glossary of the Dorset Dialect* with, as the subtitle explained 'The History and Out-spreadings and Bearings of the South-Western English.' The wording suggests a certain Saxonising element in the language of the book and, indeed, the Society agreed to publish the text only on the agreement of the author that he would Latinise much of his text as well as putting his glossary into alphabetical order. For many years after its publication, portions of the glossary were reprinted in *The Dorset County Chronicle* from time to time with the request that, should any reader be able to add to them, he should communicate with Barnes at Came.

Shortly after arriving at the Rectory, Barnes also published the third and last collection of his poems of rural life in the Dorset dialect. The hundred new poems included drew upon his now familiar themes. The standard of writing was in no way inferior to that of the two previous collections and, indeed, the book contains some of his most celebrated poems: *The Child an' the Mowers, Don't Ceare* and *John Bloom in Lon'on*. There is still no trace of his experience after leaving Blackmore save for the shadow of his wife's death over the love poems. In *Woak Hill* he transmutes that experience and his subsequent move to Came, to the thoughts of an old countryman disturbed at being made to leave the family home because his dead wife might no longer know where to find him:

> When sycamore leaves wer a-spreaden,
>   Green-ruddy, in hedges,
> Bezide the red doust o' the ridges,
>   A-dried at Woak Hill;
>
> I packed up my goods all a-sheenen
>   Wi' long years o' handlen,
> On dousty red wheels ov a waggon,
>   To ride at Woak Hill.
>
> The brown thatchen ruf o' the dwellen
>   I then wer a-leäven,
> Had shelter'd the sleek head o' Meäry,
>   My bride at Woak Hill.

But now vor zome years, her light voot-vall
    'S a-lost vrom the vlooren.
Too soon vor my jaÿ an' my children,
    She died at Woak Hill.

But still I do think that, in soul,
    She do hover about us;
To ho vor her motherless childern,
    Her pride at Woak Hill.

Zoo—lest she should tell me hereafter
    I stole off 'ithout her,
An' left her, uncall'd at house-ridden,
    To bide at Woak Hill—

I call'd her so fondly, wi' lippens
    All soundless to others,
An' took her wi' aïr-reachen hand,
    To my zide at Woak Hill.

On the road I did look round, a-talken
    To light at my shoulder,
An' then led her in at the door-way,
    Miles wide vrom Woak Hill.

An' that's why vo'k thought, vor a season,
    My mind wer a-wandren
Wi' sorrow, when I wer so sorely
    A-tried at Woak Hill.

But no; that my Meäry mid never
    Behold herzelf slighted,
I wanted to think that I guided
    My guide vrom Woak Hill.[9]

E.M. Forster said of this poem that it was impossible to read it
without tears in one's eyes. How far it is a true summary of
Barnes's emotions on leaving the old family home at South Street
is a matter of speculation, but his distress at the time must surely
have muted his joy on receiving the living of Came. Years after,
he was showing a group of visitors round the old house when,
having come to what was once 'Julia's room', he broke off his
narration and muttered that he could not go on with the visit.

Barnes always preferred what he called his 'pathetic' pieces
though his audience of the 1860's called more often for his comic
poems. He had by the early years of the decade become an expert

reader who could cunningly vary his programme and, at that time, he achieved as loyal a local following as it is possible for a poet to wish. Thereafter he wrote fewer dialect poems and his local fame diminished over the years until it was revived by the publication of *Poems of Rural Life in the Dorset Dialect* which brought together the poems of the three collections in one volume. It is this stout little book, brought out by Messrs Kegan Paul & Co., which familiarised Barnes to late Victorian readers of poetry. In practice it superseded all previous editions and was reprinted seven times, in 1883, 1886, 1888, 1893, 1898, 1902 and 1905.

His work was also well known to the firm of MacMillan for he contributed to *MacMillan's Magazine* from 1861 to 1867, and Alexander Macmillan was one of Barnes's supporters who urged him to write in standard English so that he might obtain a wider audience. Such advisers sometimes suggested Barnes should write his poems in English and others that he should 'English' his dialect poems. Macmillan is not very clear on the technique to be used but he is very sure about the reason why Barnes should attempt English poems:

'I cannot help wishing that your poems or the greater part of them could be read in ordinary English speech. I personally don't dislike a dialect and being used to the true basis of good English, the old Scottish tongue, (perhaps you won't admit this) can always make a good shot at what any word having Saxon characters in them means. But then you know it does not fall to the lot of the whole British public to have the blessings of a Scotch birth. For the sake of the unfortunates could you do something'

His old friend Charles Tennant was another siren voice urging him to forsake the dialect. Tennant encouraged him to feel that he had a contribution to make to literature even more significant than his poetry: 'Why not devote yourself to a book by which you will be remembered *as* something more than a poet ... *for* something which will make the world wiser and better than you found it?[11] Tennant did not clarify his remarks and Barnes made no great efforts to elucidate them.

It is not surprising, however, that Barnes was vulnerable to the flattery of such men as Tennant. As a writer in his sixties, with little public fame and no profit at all from over thirty books, these voices urging him to enlarge his audience, by writing in national English, were very persuasive. He once admitted that writing in dialect for an ever-diminishing rural audience was 'as idle as the writing one's name in the snow of a spring day.' He submitted to his admirers and, in 1868, Alexander Macmillan published *Poems of Rural Life in Common English*. Despite the fact that the reviewer in *The Pall Mall Gazette* described him as 'Our charming idyllist', the volume was not a success and was never reprinted.

To understand the relative failure of his English poems it is useful to compare one of them to the Dorset version of the 'same' poem.[12] The opening verses are sufficient for the purposes of comparison:

COME AND MEET ME
HUSBAND TO WIFE

Well, to-day then I shall roll off on the road
Round by Woodcombe, out to Shellbrook, to the mill;
With my brand-new little spring-cart, with a load,
To come loadless round by Chalk-hill, at my will:
As the whole day will be dry,
By the tokens of the sky,
Come to meet me, with the children, on the road.[13]

COME AN' MEET ME WI' THE CHILDREN ON THE ROAD

Well, to-day Jeäne is my set time vor to goo
To the grist-mill out at Sherbrook under Bere,
Wi' my spring-cart out in cart-house, vier new,
An' zome grist corn, to come hwomeward wi' en leer.
Zoo's the whole day will be dry,
By the readship o' the sky,
Come to meet me, wi' the children, on the road.[14]

The English verse is a competent performance, especially in the artful rhyming, but it must be admitted that it is rather tame in effect and that such lines as 'To come loadless round by Chalk-hill, at my will' are positively wooden. The lines might have been written by many nineteenth century pastoralists. The Dorset version is by comparison much more immediate and authentic. A phrase such as 'vier new' is at once colloquial and

imaginative, meaning perhaps that the brightly-painted cart has
the intensive colour of flame or that it is shod with iron hoops
straight from the smith's furnace. The effect of the dialect in the
Dorset verse is to endow its phraseology with the sanction of
long continuance and familiarity within the rural community.
Thus, the words 'to come homeward wi' en leer,' that is, to come
home with an empty wagon, must have been repeated countless
of times in rural communities and has an ease and naturalness
which is lacking in the clumsy 'to come loadless'. It is interesting
that the English poem comes fitted out with a stage direction
while the Dorset, by its employment of more intimate reference,
implies the relationship between speaker and audience and for
this reason the second version is much more dramatic. The
Dorset was for Barnes not merely an alternative mode of
expression, but a set of references, attitudes and allusions which
assumed a community of feeling and experience. As such, the
language was more intimate and precise than the more abstract
terminology adopted by the world of learning. Barnes was
frequently congratulated by expatriots upon the way that his
verse brought back for them the sense of Dorset in earlier years.
One of the most moving of these expressions of thanks came
from a servant woman now exiled from Dorset:

December 29th 1869

Reverend Sir,
    I wish you most heartily a happy New Year and hope you will excuse a
poor woman writing to you. I had to dust some books the other day that
came from a sale and amongst them was your Poems in the Dorset Dialect.
    Sir, I shook hands with you in my heart, and I laughed and cried by
turns.
    The old home of my youth and all my dear ones now mouldering in the
earth came back to mind. How happy we used to be at Christmas Time.
    And sometimes I sit down in the gloom of an underground London
Kitchen and shut my eyes and try to fancy I am on Beaminster Down
where I have spent many a happy hour years ago. But I try to think we
must be content wherever the Lord has cast our lot and not hanker for the
past. May God bless you and all yours, is the true wish of an old
Domestic Servant, who loves the very name of Dorsetshire.[15]

    One person who had never recommended the Englishing of
the poems was Coventry Patmore, poet, critic, and then assistant

librarian in the British Museum. He wrote to Barnes to declare that 'I quite agree with those who do not wish to see your poems put into London English, or anything like it. I understood them all quite well the first time I read them, though I am myself a cockney.' He had reviewed the third collection of dialect poems in both the *North British Review* and *MacMillan's Magazine,* and his favourable comments had resulted in an invitation to stay at Came. He replied to say that he was unable to come because he was unable to leave the bedside of his sick wife. After she died in 1862 he accepted.

Patmore felt that he had much in common with Barnes. They had both been left widowers with six children to look after, they were both poets, devout Christians and lovers of natural beauty. He wrote in July 1863 to finalise his visit. He would come with his daughter; little walks would not content him for he professed to be a 'great walker' and this would relieve Barnes and Laura of entertaining him. He wished, he declared, to visit the haunts of Barnes's 'Blackmore Maidens', which sentiment must have occasioned some unease at the Rectory, both on account of Patmore's knowledge of Dorset geography, and on the value of his expressions of eternal fidelity to his late wife.

For Patmore was best known to the reading public as a sort of professional poetic husband. His poem *Angel in the House* had appeared in its final form in 1863 and the second volume, containing the part known as 'Faithful for Ever', had been so popular with lovers of the poetry of sentimental domesticity that it had sold a quarter of a million copies. Patmore's stimulus was in recollections of his life with his dead wife and his mystical belief that they would be reunited in heaven. He wanted to talk about poetry and mystical unions with Barnes but, to his disappointment, his host encouraged no such talk. The Barnes daughters professed themselves to be great admirers of *The Angel in the House,* which must have seemed to them to be in accord with their father's profound feeling for his own dead wife. Barnes, however, refused to be drawn on such matters. Patmore complained: 'I wanted to discuss the mystery of the Incarnation and I found Barnes buried in a horrible kind of thing called TIW'. Barnes's scholarship was rather a barrier to any development of the relationship, as Patmore had anticipated when he wrote to Barnes before the visit to express his considerable degree of awe 'at having committed myself to becoming the guest of one who is so notable a scholar as well as a great poet. I am an ignoramus and have read little out of my own language and not much in that.'[16] The visit was not a success and did not lead to a lasting friendship. Barnes was never one for mysticism and may have found Patmore's expressions of undying love for his wife just too much of a good thing. About a year later, William Allingham concluded a letter to Barnes with a PS: 'A murmur says that Patmore is about to marry a rich Italian lady, and has turned Catholic!' Both rumours turned out to be true and, indeed, Patmore was three times married in his lifetime. It may have been religious differences or the suspicion that Patmore's expressions of conjugal fidelity were not wholehearted that diminished Barnes's opinion of him. Patmore, on the other hand, retained an affection for Barnes till the end, and begged Gosse to remember him to the Dorset poet when the latter was on his deathbed over twenty years after the visit.

Patmore's visit was the first of a number of pilgrimages paid to Came Rectory by figures of literary note. In May, 1864, another visitor was the Irish poet, William Allingham, confidant of the Poet Laureate, Lord Tennyson, and later better known as the author of the poem *The Fairies* which begins 'Up the airy mountain, Down the rushy glen . . .'

Allingham's visit was repaid in November of the same year when Barnes went to Lymington in Hampshire. Allingham was a diarist to rival Kilvert, and his account of the meeting is worthy of record:

'Rev William Barnes comes on my invitation to give a lecture at the Literary Institute – He duly arrives by train at 3, and I gladly welcome the good old poet. We walk about the town, and he shows much interest in the shops, old china, pictures, etc., and bargains for a little oil painting. Aide himself arrives, whom I have invited to meet Barnes. I take them for a walk to Buckland Rings, supposed Ancient British Camp; then dinner at my lodgings (which I hope went off tolerably), and he moved to the Lecture Room. Mr Barnes lectured on 'West of England Speech', and read some of his own poems. What the audience liked best was 'A Bit of Sly Coortin'.' which he gave at my request. It was excellent . . . in comparison with the paid entertainers who occasionally come round . . .

Wednesday Nov 2nd – Wm. Barnes: he praised my Stratford-on-Avon dialogue, suggested some points of dialect, but does not understand the Warwickshire. I saw him into the train at 1.40. A man of simple manners and virtuous life, and a true poet. Though he is so much my elder, I was one of the first to make a stir about him, in talk and by the Press. The Brownings, Tennyson, Clough, Rossetti, etc., etc. – it was I who introduced Barnes's Dorset poems to each and all of them.

I met in the street old 'Lawyer M' who said he had been at the lecture last night, and 'thought it the damndest stuff he had ever heard' to which I made brief reply.'[17]

Barnes paid a further visit to Lymington in 1865 when he lectured on 'House and Housewife'. Allingham recollected that he spoke of 'caves, huts, tents, etc., Wives (laughter), praise of the good wife' in a lecture that rather puzzled everybody.[18] On the following day, Barnes went with Allingham across on the ferry to the Isle of Wight, where they paid a visit to Lord Alfred Tennyson at his home at Farringford. Long after, Allingham retained a picture of Barnes sitting on the boat, with his 'old fashioned ways' . . . 'his gaiters, his long-knitted purse, which he ties up in a knot, broad brimmed hat, homely speech.' After landing at Yarmouth, they drove in a fly to Farringford:

where T., Mrs T., Miss T. meet us in the hall. T. and B. at once on easy terms, having simple poetic minds and mutual goodwill. Talk of Ancient Britons, barrows, roads, etc. I to upper room and dress, T. comes in to me and we go down together. Dinner: stories of ghosts and dreams. To drawing-room as usual, where T. has his port, B. no wine. T. says: 'modern fame is nothing: I'd rather have an acre of land. I shall go down, down! I am up now.' T. went upstairs by himself.

Julia Margaret Cameron, the photographer, was a neighbour of Tennyson's and came in for tea. Tennyson refused her request to go to her studio the next day to be photographed and suggested Barnes instead. Mrs Cameron declined the suggestion on the ground that Barnes's head was not sufficiently impressive. Allingham recorded her departure:

T. and I went out to the porch with Mrs C., where her donkey-chaise was waiting in the moonlight.

Tennyson now took Barnes and me to his top room. Darwinism – 'Man from ape – would that really make any difference?' Huxley, Tyndall.

'Time is nothing,' said T., 'are we not all part of Deity?' 'Pantheism?'
hinted Barnes, who was not at ease in this sort of speculation. 'Well!'
says T., 'I think I believe in Pantheism, of a sort.' Barnes to bed.[19]

When they were alone, Tennyson confided to Allingham that he
liked Barnes but thought that he was not 'accustomed to strong
views theologic'.

There was a last magical meeting between the three poets one
late August night in 1867. Answering a rap at the Rectory door,
Barnes found, to his amazement, Tennyson and Allingham on
the step. Allingham takes up the story:

'The twilight being fine I propose that we should visit William Barnes
whom T. personally knows and whose poems in the Dorset dialect T
knows and likes. I show the way to Came Vicarage, where I had enjoyed
hospitality from Saturday to Monday a year or two before. The cottage-
parsonage lies in a hollow among trees about a mile from Dorchester,
separated from the public road by a little grass plot and shrubbery. We
find the gate by starlight and reach the house door before 9 or 10 o'clock.
The worthy old Poet-Vicar is truly delighted to see us, especially such a
guest as T (whose poetry, he used to say, has 'heart-tone' in it).
    Barnes himself lets us in and comes out at once into the passage –
'Here's an honour.' Little Miss Barnes and Mrs Shaw, a married
daughter, appear, B. says 'put out something', 'put out something with
hospitable fervour, tho' we lack no bodily refreshment. Barnes himself,
by the way, though not a teetotaller, is an abstemious man, very plain
and inexpensive in his diet. We are pressed to stay but can't . . .[20]

So the three poets ate and talked together. Tennyson told tales of
his servant who styled himself 'The King of Connaught'. Then
Barnes took his hat and, at the age of sixty-seven, walked out into
the early morning starlight and accompanied them to the edge of
Dorchester. When he turned back for the Rectory, they pursued
their walk which was to take them all the way down to Lyme
Regis, where they next called upon Francis Turner Palgrave. So
impressed was Tennyson with the dialect poetry of Barnes, that
he himself tried his hand in the dialect of his own native Lincolnshire, and wrote two poems entitled 'The Northern Farmer.'

Barnes's spare hours were given now more to study than to
poetry. Philology was still his first love but it was followed closely
by early history and a general interest in antiquities. In 1869 he
published *Early England and the Saxon English* which provided a

sympathetic account of the race which Barnes considered to be the ancestors of his Blackmore folk, but also included a renewed plea for a purification of the English language from Latin and French importations.

Throughout Dorset and beyond, Barnes's advice was now often sought on archaeological and antiquarian matters so that, when the Dorset Field Club was formed in 1873, he became a founder member and leading figure in the enterprise. For the next few years he attended 'digs' and field meetings, until advancing age prevented it, but even then he kept up to date in archaeology by avidly reading the journals of the various societies. Nothing, however, could keep him from the opening of the new premises of the County Museum in 1881. The Museum still occupies the site at the junction of South Street and High West Street, adjacent to St Peter's Church, where Barnes's statue now stands.

Yet it was Barnes's poetry that gained him most admirers. In the 1860's a selection of the early dialect poems and some of the English poems were published in Boston, recruiting him an American readership. From that time he received occasional letters of admiration and even visitors from the United States. In 1870, an American poet named Moncure Conway visited him at the Rectory and published a sentimentalised account of his visit in *Harper's Magazine*. Barnes corresponded with a Mr Otis on the subject of Dorset folklore and with the poet, Daniel Ricketson of New Bedford, who wrote movingly in 1879 to say how he wished to visit old Dorset again but feared that he was too infirm to do so. This notice taken of his work by 'Darzet Vo'k Across the Zeas' afforded the aged poet much innocent pleasure. One item that especially intrigued him was a letter dated May 17th 1882, the first typed item that he had ever received. It came from Messrs J.M. Stoddart, publishers of Philadelphia, who informed him that they were seeking information on 'persons of note still living' for the American supplement to the *Encyclopaedia Brittanica*, an assurance that must have occasioned mixed feelings in the poet. One letter, however, came too late to afford him any pleasure. Six months before his death in 1886, Barnes received a letter from Ben W. Stone, the Hon Secretary of the North Western Literary and Historical Society of Sioux City, Iowa, who wrote to

say that his members had unanimously elected Barnes an hono-
rary member 'as an expression of their recognition of his beautiful verses and great learning.'

Barnes's last two philological books were more than ever concerned to demonstrate the adequacy and effectiveness of 'pure
English', i.e. that free of Latinisms and based upon the old Saxon
speech of Blackmore. *An Outline of Speech-Craft* appeared in 1878
and lists a set of 'English' replacements for Latin terms. For
example, he suggests that 'Aeronaut', 'Aerology' and 'Ambi-
guous' should be replaced by 'Air-farer', 'Air-lore' and 'Twy-
sided'.

In 1880 Barnes published *An Outline of Rede-Craft (Logic) with
English Wording*, which, as its title suggests, is a textbook of logic
written entirely in 'pure', i.e. Saxon, English. The intention of
the writer was to demonsrate that even a subject as difficult and
abstract as logic could be explained comprehensibly in Saxon
English. The result presented contemporary readers with some
of the oddest prose produced in the nineteenth century: 'If he
wants to bring out an unstraitened ayesome up-shot, the
middle-step-end may be the fore-end to the higher step, and
hinder end to the lower step.'[21] *The Athenaeum* dismissed the
book as the work of an 'enthusiast' and no other journal reviewed
it. Some modern readers have defended the book by pointing
out that, if it is difficult to understand, then so is any book on
logic, and also that the prose becomes more comprehensible the
more one perseveres with it. Nevertheless, the language of the
Outline of Redecraft is a strange land which few have chosen to
explore.

Despite his undoubted erudition and industry as a philologist,
Barnes did not achieve a national reputation in the field as did
his contemporaries, Sweet, Skeat and Furnivall. The focus for
English philological research was the Philological Society which,
in 1863, published Barnes's *Grammar & Glossary* but which never
invited him to become a member. The great work of the Society
was the preparation of its dictionary, which was eventually
published as *The Oxford English Dictionary* in 1888, two years
after Barnes's death. In their prospectus, the editors of the *Dictionary* declared the principle that there should be no exclusions
on the grounds of 'obsoleteness, foreignness or localism'[22], yet

they almost completely ignored the hundreds of revived terms or neologisms suggested by Barnes in his various publications.

The Hon Secretary and driving force of the Society was F.J. Furnivall and there can be little doubt that it was he who decided that Barnes's dialect terms were not to appear in the *Dictionary*. It may well have been that Furnivall considered Barnes's determination to 'purify' English as the attitude of a crank.[23] The grand design of restoring English to its Saxon origins struck even such an admirer as Gerard Manley Hopkins as not entirely level-headed. After having perused Barnes's *Speech-Craft* in 1882, he wrote to Robert Bridges: 'In fact I am learning Anglo-Saxon and it is a vastly superior thing to what we have now. But the madness of an almost unknown man trying to do what three estates of the realm together could never accomplish!'[24]

Few poets enjoy the serenity which came to Barnes in old age. His days were spent visiting parishioners, conducting services at Whitcombe or Came, digging in the garden, working at his philology, attending site meetings of the Dorset Field Club, and wandering in his garden where two stone lions crouched on either side of his gravel path. Laura and Isabel were his house-keepers and 'curates' until the latter's marriage to a London solicitor, T.G. Gardner, in 1882. William's six children were frequent visitors to their grandfather and, during the summer months, there were also grandchildren from Italy or visiting children, such as the Powys brothers and the young John Meade Falkner, author of *Moonfleet*.

The white-bearded, softly-spoken old poet was a picture of old-world gallantry to the many young girls invited by his daughters or grand-daughters. He called them 'maidens' and invented names for them such as 'the light of the house' and 'the gliding cypress'. He still walked his parish whatever the weather. In February, 1881, for example, he set out to preach at Came by 9 o'clock, met someone begging him to attend a dying woman at Whitcombe, held the service at Came, walked to the other end of the parish to conduct the service for the dying, walked home again, ate a hasty lunch, then returned to Came to take a funeral and conduct Evensong. He was eighty years old and had walked over fifteen miles on snow-covered roads, had taken two services, a wedding, a funeral and an office for the sick all on one day.[25]

The walk from east to west across his parish would bring him at lunch-time to Herringston House, the Tudor mansion which was the home of the Williams family and which he had celebrated in a poem. Here lunch was kept for him and, after his death, his hostess, Mrs Sophia Williams, wrote a memorial of him in a letter to William Miles:

'He was a delightful companion and among our large family party of all ages there was not one but felt this. The wonderful range of his information accounted for the interest of his conversation, but I think its great charm lay in his own perfect simplicity, and enjoyment of the talk of others; his hearers always felt that they were talked *with* not *to*. His quaint modes of expression gave point to all he said, and his infectious laugh when he told a story of any of his people, especially if it told against himself, with the dry, 'Ah, she (or he) was too sharp for me there,' comes back to me as I write this . . .'[26]

A guest of the Williams had once expressed herself afraid to meet anyone so learned as Barnes, but one of the children had replied indignantly 'But no one was ever afraid of Mr Barnes.' In fact he was a popular favourite with the cottagers and their children throughout the parish. One woman confided to Lucy Baxter that they told their Rector their troubles as freely as if he had been their mother, while the children clustered around him as he went from home to home to obtain the sweetmeats he kept in his pocket for the purpose. Herringston was halfway across his parish and he would usually conclude his day's walk by calling at his son's rectory, at Monkton, where he would be greeted by welcoming shouts from his grandchildren, and where he would take tea before starting for home.

The Rectory at Came continued to be a place of pilgrimage for the literary world until Barnes's death. Martin Tupper, the author of the popular verses of the *Proverbial Philosophy* called in 1866, while Francis Kilvert's famous visit took place in April 1874. Another visitor, then in his late teens, was Arthur Quiller-Couch, who was to become the first Professor of English Literature at Cambridge University, and who gave a description of the visit in a lecture published some fifty years after:

The house straw-thatched – rioted over by creepers – was set around with trees. Swallows populated its eaves; bees hummed in its garden. I am painting you (however you suspect it) no nook of fancy, but the residence of an actual man, whom you will find at once idyllic shrewd and solid. He is just past eighty, but hale yet, white bearded with an aspect which suggests what you can recollect of Saint Mark from any number of stained glass windows. His hair, too, is white and he wears it patriarchally long so that it touches his shoulders. He is dressed in a long black coat, knee-breeches, black stockings, stout buckled shoes. He has a rustic pair of shoulders, with a scholar's stoop; and his tunable voice, after greeting, will continue in the accent of educated English or slide into broad Doric unconsciously as he admits you to intimacy. You will be made welcome within the Rectory, the downstairs living room of which consists of a dark little dining room lined with books; a bright parlour, a trifle overcrowded with "works of art" – some of home manufacture, others picked up on his rare peregrinations, long since forsworn; last, a small study, in which he shuts himself up of an evening, only to be tempted forth when his two daughters close the day with music and voice in the outer room. These are his "blest pair of Sirens" (at what cost of self-abregation, taken for granted in those days, we must not enquire).[27]

Another visitor was Thomas Hardy whom Barnes had known since he was a boy of sixteen. After the publication of *Far From the Madding Crowd*, Hardy had given up architecture to become a full-time writer. Now, in 1883, as a married man of 43 years old, he had taken lodgings in Dorchester while awaiting the completion of his new home at Max Gate. This house, which he had designed for himself, lay on the Dorchester to Broadmayne road, just round the corner from Came Rectory. There were also a shorter path through the fields connecting the two houses. Thus, when Hardy entered into his new home and was concluding *The Mayor of Casterbridge*, he was in almost daily contact with Barnes for the last two year's of the poet's life, despite differences in religious outlook and in age.

It was Hardy who introduced Barnes to Edmund Gosse whom he brought to the Rectory on 22nd July, 1883. He had written to Barnes earlier, requesting to introduce Gosse whom he described as 'one of your sincerest admirers'. Gosse left a record of the visit and it is clear that, though Barnes offered them both a hearty welcome, he was not disposed to scamp parish duties to greet guests, however eminent:

Hardy and I walked last afternoon through fields of rye 5 or even 6 feet high to the village of Winterborne Came of which Mr Barnes the poet is Rector. We were ushered up to the choir, behind a delicious old carved screen, among 17th century marble monuments of the Earls of Portarlinton.

The church is a tiny little affair, that you could put in your pocket, the congregation seemed to fill it pretty well, and yet we were only 45 souls in all. Barnes is a wonderful figure, he is in his 83rd year. He has long, thin, silky hair flowing down and mingling with a full beard and moustache almost as white as milk, a grand dome of forehead over a long, thin, pendulous nose, not at all a handsome face, but full of intelligence, and a beauty of vigour in extreme old age. He undertook the entire service himself and preached rather a long sermon. Then he stayed behind to hear the school-children practice their singing and walked to the Rectory as he had walked from it, rather over a mile. We waited in Came Park and he caught us up.[28]

There is a certain delicate irony in the situation when it is appreciated that this pious old man, whom Llewelyn Powys called 'the last of the believers', should give priority to the taking of choir practice, before turning to entertain his guests, one of whom was the most eminent sceptic among nineteenth century novelists, and the other of whom was to publish *Father & Son* in 1907, in which he was so successfully to articulate his rejection of Christian faith.

In the summer of 1883 it became apparent to Barnes's children that their father's great strength was failing and so they tried to tempt him away from his work by suggesting various holiday schemes. He rejected them all until they suggested a trip to Blackmore, an idea he found irresistible. One summer's day, William and his family took 'grandfather' to Sturminster Newton where the old man was able to identify the familiar spots of his boyhood. Here again were the banks of the Stour, the shining waters and the clumps of 'clotes' he had loved as a boy; here was the school he had attended, now converted to a carpenter's shop; here was the market square where he had once deliberately stampeded a herd of cows and been chased by the farmer. In the afternoon, the family was lent a boat, and even the elderly poet took turns in steering as they glided among the meadows where he and Charlie Rabbetts had run and shouted together seventy years before.

This was Barnes's last trip away from home. On the morning of January 26th, 1884, a sudden chill rainstorm broke swiftly over the road out of Dorchester as Hardy and Barnes were walking home. Hardy begged Barnes to take shelter at Max Gate but the old Rector persisted in walking on so that, when he arrived home, he had to go to bed with a chill. From that day his health declined and he suffered from rheumatic troubles and a general failing. He found that his attempts to continue with parish work were more and more exhausting though he did manage to take Holy Communion at Came on March 9th, 1884. On February 15th of the following year he took his last service, at Whitcombe, where he had begun his ministry. Gosse wrote to Patmore to tell him about the appearance of his old friend:

Hardy and I went on Monday last to Came Rectory where he lies bedridden. We found him in bed in his study, his face turned to the window, where the light came streaming in through flowering plants, his brown books on all sides of him save one, the wall behind him being hung with an old green tapestry. He had a scarlet bedgown on, a kind of soft biretta of dark red wool on his head, from which his long white hair escaped onto the pillow; his grey beard, grown very long, upon his breast; his complexion, which you recollect as richly bronzed, has become blanched by keeping indoors, and is now waxily white where it is not waxily pink, the blue eyes, half shut, restless under languid lids . . . I wish I could paint for you the strange effect of this old, old man, lying in cardinal scarlet in his white bed, the only bright spot in the gloom of all those books. You must think that I make too much of these outer signs, but it seemed to me that this unconscious mise-en-scène in the solitude of this out-of-the-way Rectory was very curious and characteristic.[29]

Laura was now helped to nurse her father by a family friend named Miss Benson. In October, 1885, he rallied a little and was able to sit by the fireside listening to the sounds of the house. He had always disliked the sound of the wicket gate closing. On hearing it one day, he asked Laura to take dictation from him and she wrote:

THE GEATE A-VALLEN TO

In the zunsheen ov our zummers
    Wi' the haÿ time now a-come,
How busy wer we out a-vield
    Wi' view a-left at hwome,
When waggons rumbled out ov yard
    Red wheeled, wi' body blue,
As back behind 'em loudly slamm'd
The geäte a-vallen to.

Drough daysheen ov how many years
    The geäte ha' now a-swung
Behind the veet o' vull-grown men
    An' vootsteps ov the young.
Drough years o' days it swung to us
    Behind each little shoe,
As we tripped lightly on avore
    The geäte a-vallen to.

In evenen time o' starry night
    How mother zot at hwome,
An' kept her bleäzen vire bright
    Till father should ha' come,
An' how she quicken'd up an' smiled
    An' stirred her vire anew,
To hear the trampen ho'ses' steps
    An' geäte a-vallen to.

There's moon-sheen now in nights o' fall
    When leaves be brown vrom green,
When, to the slammen o' the geäte,
    Our Jenny's ears be keen,
When the wold dog do wag his taïl,
    An' Jeän could tell to who,
As he do come in drough the geäte,
    The geäte a-vallen to.

An' oft do come a saddened hour
    When there must goo away
One well-beloved to our heart's core,
    Vor long, perhaps vor aye:
An' oh! it is a touchen thing
    The loven heart must rue,
To hear behind his last farewell
    The geäte a-vallen to.[30]

After the dictation he seemed full of foreboding but also given to musing on the words he had just uttered. He bade Laura mark the spelling of the word 'geate'; "that he said, is how King Alfred would have pronounced it."

At Christmas 1885 he was too weak to go downstairs to join in the festivities but, instead, blessed every member of the family and the household servants as they came to his room. Isabel visited him with her new husband; Colonel Damer called in from Came House; as did Hardy, Gosse and Bishop Wordsworth of Salisbury. The present that had meant most to him had arrived early, in November, when the author's copy of his new edition of the *Glossary of the Dorset Dialect* had been placed in his hand. For over twenty years he had supplemented his previous collection with Dorset expressions contributed by readers of *The Dorset County Chronicle*. This book, more than any other, preserved a permanent record of the fast-dying native speech of his county. Here at least the curious reader of future days could learn that a bumblebee was once known as a 'dumbledore' in Dorset, that a scarecrow was referred to as a 'mammet' and that a lazy boy on the farm was said to 'loppy about'. In preserving the language, Barnes had saved something of the life of Blackmore days.

Laura Barnes described how he died. On the night of 6th October, 1886, he had awakened from sleep in a cheerful frame of mind and repeated with her from the Prayer Book 'Lighten our darkness we beseech thee, O Lord.' The next day he asked for the lessons of the day to be read to him. Between twelve and one o'clock he drowsed and then, in a low voice thanked God for all the pains and trials he had passed. In the afternoon Laura dozed a little in the parlour but was awakened by the sounds of William and Emily arriving. When they went to the bedroom they found their father dead. He had died peacefully in his sleep.[31]

The funeral took place on October 11th at Came. It was a day of dark cloud as the coffin was wheeled on a little hand-cart, out of the now opened gate at the Rectory, into the main road and then down the track to the church. It was followed by William Miles and his family, Laura, Isabel and her husband, Professor Palgrave and his son and the local people from the parish. The *County Chronicle* reported:

'On the coffin being lowered to its last resting place it was literally covered with beautiful wreaths and crosses sent by loving friends and parishioners ... The schoolchildren of Came, with Miss Foot, the mistress, were present and dropped flowers, chiefly wild, into the grave.'[32]

Thomas Hardy must have been a little late for the funeral as he was just leaving Max Gate when the elm coffin was pushed out onto the road below. As he looked down to the road in the darkness of the year something seemed to flash before his eyes. He knew what it was:

THE LAST SIGNAL

(Oct. 11, 1886)

A MEMORY OF WILLIAM BARNES

Silently I footed by an uphill road
That led from my abode to a spot yew-boughed;
Yellowly the sun sloped low down to westward,
    And dark was the east with cloud.

Then, amid the shadow of that livid sad east,
Where the light was least, and a gate stood wide,
Something flashed the fire of the sun that was facing it,
    Like a brief blaze on that side.

Looking hard and harder I knew what it meant—
The sudden shine sent from the livid east scene;
It meant the west mirrored by the coffin of my friend there,
    Turning to the road from his green,

To take his last journey forth – he who in his prime
Trudged so many a time from that gate athwart the land!
Thus a farewell to me he signalled on his grave-way;
    As with a wave of his hand.

Winterborne Came Path.[33]

Further Reading and Notes

LIFE

Hardy, Thomas 'The Reverend William Barnes B.D.', in *The Athenaeum*, for 16th October, 1886, reprinted in Orel, Harold, *Thomas Hardy's Personal Writings*, MacMillan, 1967, pp100-106.

Baxter, Lucy ('Leader Scott'), *The Life of William Barnes Poet & Philologist*, MacMillan, 1887

Dugdale, Giles, *William Barnes of Dorset*, Cassell & Co., 1953

Levy, William Turner, *William Barnes: The Man & His Poems*, Longmans (Dorchester), 1960

Hearl, Trevor W., *William Barnes the Schoolmaster*, Longmans, (Dorchester), 1966

POEMS

Hardy, Thomas, (Ed.) *Select Poems of William Barnes*, Henry Froude, 1908

Dugdale, Giles, *Poems Grave & Gay by William Barnes*, Longmans (Dorchester), 1949

Grigson, G., *Selected Poems of William Barnes*, Routledge & Kegan Paul, 1950

Jones, Bernard, (Ed.) *The Poems of William Barnes*, in two vols., Southern Illinois University Press, 1962

Chedzoy, Alan, *Poems Grave & Gay by William Barnes*, Friary Press, (Dorchester), 1978

Wrigley, Chris, *William Barnes the Dorset Poet*, The Dovecote Press, 1984

CRITICISM

Hardy, Thomas, 'Poems of Rural Life in the Dorset Dialect', unsigned review in the *New Quarterly Magazine*, October, 1879, reprinted in Orel, pp94-100.

Forster, E.M., 'William Barnes' in *Two Cheers for Democracy*, 1951, reprinted by Edward Arnold in 1972

Quiller-Couch, Sir Arthur, 'William Barnes' in *The Poet as Citizen*, Cambridge University Press, 1934.

Abbott, Claude Colleer, *Further Letters of Gerard Manley Hopkins*, Oxford University Press, 1970.

Larkin, Philip, 'The Poetry of William Barnes' in *Required Writing*, Faber & Faber, 1983

There is an extensive critical literature on Barnes's poetry, and the list above includes only the essential items. Lucy Baxter's book must be the starting point for all biographers of the poet but the outstanding piece of research is Trevor Hearl's study, though, as its title indicates, it is restricted to Barnes's career as a teacher. Both Dugdale and Hearl list Barnes's own publications, including the important contributions to the *Gentleman's Magazine, MacMillan's Magazine* and other journals.

The word 'Dugdale' in the notes below indicates *William Barnes of Dorset.* Other abbreviations are as follows:

DCM   Dorset County Museum
DCL   Dorset County Library
DCRO   Dorset County Record Office
PDNC   *Proceedings of the Dorset Natural History and Antiquarian Field Club*
GM   *The Gentleman's Magazine*
MM   *MacMillan's Magazine*
DCC   *Dorset County Chronicle*

NOTES

INTRODUCTION

1 – See Hardy, Thomas, 'The Reverend William Barnes B.D.' from the *Athenaeum,* for October, 16th, 1886, in Orel
2 – See Jones, passim.

CHAPTER 1

1 – Plomer, William, *Kilvert's Diary,* Penguin Books, 1977, p.256
2 – Ibid. p258
3 – Hardy, Thomas, Op.Cit.
4 – Hardy, Thomas, *Tess of the D'Urbervilles,* 1891, chapter 2
5 – See the *Register for Baptisms for Sturminster Newton,* 1707-1808, DCRO
6 – Mr Duffett's testimony is reported in the *Western Gazette,* September 16th, 1983
7 – See Bettey, J.H., *Rural Life in Wessex 1500-1900,* Moonraker Press, Bradford-on-Avon, 1977, pp64-6.
8 – Dugdale p.7
9 – Jones I pp.314-5
10 – Ibid. I p.167
11 – Ibid. I p.202
12 – Ibid. I p.408
13 – Ibid. I p.329
14 – Ibid. I p.210

15 – Ibid. I p.108
16 – Ibid. I p.347
17 – Ibid. I p.120
18 – See Hutchinson, Thomas (Ed.), *The Poetical Works of Wordsworth*, Oxford University Press, 1960, p.590 'The Prelude' 1, lines 559-566, 581-586.
19 – Udal, John Symonds, *Dorsetshire Folklore*, Stephen Austin & Sons, 1922 repr. Toucan Press, 1970 p.2
20 – Jones I p.224
21 – Ibid I p.493
22 – Dugdale p.24
23 – See Morshead, Sir Owen, *The Story of the Parish Church of St Mary, Sturminster Newton*, pp.6-12
24 – Baxter p.11
25 – Hearl pp.13-14
26 – From *Hone's Year Book*, 1832, reprinted in Udal, op.cit.
27 – Jones 1 p.234
28 – Hardy, Thomas, *Jude the Obscure*, (1895), chapter 1 iii

CHAPTER 2

1 – See Treves, Sir Frederick, *Highways & Byways in Dorset*, Macmillan, 1906, p.358
2– and 3 The most vivid of all evocations of 19th century Dorchester are to be found in Hardy's *The Mayor of Casterbridge*, (1886) from which some of these details have been taken. See chapters IV, IX and XI
4 – Baxter p.14
5 – Jones I p.25
6 – Ibid. I p.25
7 – Ibid. I p.25
8 – Ibid. I p.27
9 – Ibid. I p.44
10 – Ibid. I pp.38-9
11 – Baxter, p.16
12 – See Oliver, Vere L. *The Late Rev. William Barnes as Engraver*, Dorset Natural History and Archaeological Society, Dorchester, 1925, p.3
13 – Ibid.
14 – Dugdale p.48

CHAPTER 3

1 – See the letter in the DCM from Barnes to Julia Miles dated 8th April, 1826. The Market House was falling into use in Barnes's day and was partially demolished in 1863. The site is now occupied by a town clock presented in 1868 by the then Prince of Wales, later Edward VIIth.
2 – See *Mere: A Wiltshire Town*, Blackmore Press, 1975, pp.69-70

3 – Jones I p.55
4 – The letter between Barnes and Julia Miles are preserved in DCM.
5 – Jones I p.55
6 – Ibid. p.58
7 – Ibid. pp.53-4
8 – See *Mere: A Wiltshire Town*
9 – Jones II p.686
10 – The chessmen with board thought to have been carved by Barnes are now in DCM.
11 – See Wallis, C.J. 'The Early Manhood of William Barnes the Dorset Poet' in GM. July, 1888, pp.23-4
12 – GM December, 1832, p.525

CHAPTER 4

1 – See Horn, Pamela, *The Rural World 1780-1850*, Hutchinson, 1980, pp.71-2.
   2 – Bettey, Op.Cit. p.117
   3 – See Marlow, Joyce, *The Tolpuddle Martyrs*, Panther, 1871, p.25
   4 – DCRO Maps of Sturminster Newton area for 1830 and 1840. A splendid account of the Swing riots in Blackmore is provided in Kerr, Joyce, *Bound to the Soil*, John Baker, 1968, chapter V.
5 – Jones I p.190
6 – See Barnes, William, *Views of Labour & Gold*, J.R. Smith, 1859.
7 – DCM Barnes scrapbook I p.17
8 – The dating of these early eclogues is significant in that it documents Barnes's response to contemporary events. Baxter's account of publication dates is both vague and inaccurate, while Dugdale merely repeats her statements. The actual dates of publication in the DCC are:

   2/1 /1834   'Rusticus Dolens or Inclosures of Common'
   9/1 /1834   'Rusticus Gaudens – The allotment System
   3/4 /1834   'Rusticus Narrans – A Cousin Down from London'
   20/11/1834   'Rusticus Emigrans – Emigration'
   25/12/1834   'Rusticus Rixans – The Best Man in the Field'
   5/2 /1835   'Rusticus Domi-Father Come Home'

Barnes subsequently changed the poems slightly by rendering their wording even further into dialect. The titles appearing in Jones are, therefore, slightly different, e.g. 'Inclosures of Common' becomes 'The Common a took In' (See Jones 1 p.158).
9 – Jones 1 p.93
10 – DCC 19/8/1830
11 – See Lewis, C. Day, *The Eclogues, Georgics and Aeneid of Virgil*, OUP, 1979, p.36
12 – GM, *April*, 1832, an article entitled 'Songs of the Ancient Romans'

13 – Jones I p.93
14 – See *The Story of the Dorchester Labourers*, TUC, 1957
15 – Hearl p.111
16 – Jones I p.226
17 – Ibid. I p.482
18 – DCC 25/12/1834
19 – Jones I p.182
20 – DCC 5/12/1835
21 – Jones I pp.306-7
22 – Ibid. I p.96

CHAPTER 5

1 – The exact location of Barnes's school in Durngate Street from 1835-7 is not known but there is some evidence to suggest that it was on the corner of Durngate Street and Church Lane. The 1810 map of Dorchester shows a property on that corner belonging to 'Robert Williams' whereas Norman House, in South Street, belong to 'Wm. Williams Esq.' As Barnes moved from one street to the other, such a move would have been facilitated, and possibly, suggested by the landlord, if both houses were in the same family. See map in DCRO.
2 – DCM Scrapbook 1 p.21
3 – Ibid. p.22
4 – Baxter, p.48
5 – See 'In Memoriam: Rev William Barnes B.D.' by Octavius Pickard Cambridge in PDNC, Vol VIII, 1887, p.xxvi.
6 – Baxter p.49
7 – Ibid. pp.49-50
8 – Ibid. p.210
9 – DCM Scrapbook 1 p.24
10 – See Jones 11 p.690 and p.841
11 – Baxter p.66
12 – Jones 1 p.207
13 Hearl p.201
14 – GM June 1838 pp.593-5
15 Pickard Cambridge, Op.Cit., xvii
16 – GM January 1841 pp.22-4
17 – MM November 1866 p.80
18 – The Museum was chosen as the setting for Hardy's *A Group of Noble Dames* (1891); He describes the members waiting in their room where the autumn firelight threw coats of mail, weapons and missals ... while the dead eyes of the stuffed birds ... flashed.' No doubt part of this collection was made by Barnes.
19 – GM February 1839 p.114
20 – Hearl p.117

21 – The name 'Maskew' was chosen by John Meade Falkner as that of the villain in his popular romance *Moonfleet* (1898). Falkner admired Barnes and, indeed, played in the garden of Came Rectory as a child. Perhaps the choice of this name for a fictional villain was a kind of literary revenge.

22 – Baxter pp.108-9

23 – Levy p.135

24 – Hearl pp.202-205

25 – Jones 1 p.334

CHAPTER 6

1 – See the 'Dissertation' to the *Poems of Rural Life in the Dorset Dialect*, John Russell Smith, London, and George Simonds, Dorchester, 1844, p.1

2 – See Hardy, Thomas 'The Dorsetshire Labourer' in *Longman's Magazine* for July 1883, reprinted in Orel, op.cit. pp.168-191.

3 – 'Dissertation' to *Poems of Rural Life*

4 – The DCM possesses two editions of the *Poems of Rural Life* (second edition), one dated 1847 and the other 1848.

5 – DCC 16/5/1844

6 – Jones 1 p.88. According to Barnes's *Glossary of the Dorset Dialect*, a 'crowd' is a fiddle, while the 'tides' or times of the year 'were formerly given by the times of some of our great fairs.'

7 – Jones 1 pp73-4. Lady Day, Old Style, was April 6th, when such removals took place. See Hardy in Orel, op.cit., pp.176-80, also Orel's note p.275.

8 – Jones 1 pp.194-5

9 – Ibid. I p.198

10 – See Grigson G. (Ed.), *William Allingham's Diary*, Centaur Press, Fontwell, 1967 p.109.

11 – See Levy pp.160-164, for an account of Barnes's metrical experiments.

12 – Jones 1 p.86

13 – See Hardy, Thomas, Preface to his *Select Poems of William Barnes* 1908 pp.ix & x.

14 – See Grigson G. (ed.) Introduction to *Selected Poems of William Barnes* pp.10-11.

15 – DCC 16/4/1844 and 16/10/1844

316 – *The Sherborne and Yeovil Mercury*, December 1844

17 – GM December 1844

18 – Jones 11 p.693

19 – Baxter p.242

20 –Jones 11 p.643

CHAPTER 7

1 – Jones 1 pp.513-4. An interesting echo of this phrase is to be found in Chapter XVIII of *The Mayor of Casterbridge*: 'And all her shining keys will be took from her . . .'

2 – Baxter pp.109-110

3 – Baxter p.110

4 – No copy of *The Outline of Geography* is known to exist.

5 – Barnes's copy of Richards's notebook has recently been discovered and purchased for DCRO.

6 – See the *Retrospective Review*, Vol 1, August, 1853, pp.417-418.

7 – Middle-class Dorchester parents were concerned as others elsewhere that their children should discard any traces of local dialect described by Hardy as 'those terrible marks of the beast to the truly genteel'. In Chapter XX of *The Mayor of Casterbridge*, Henchard chides Elizabeth Jane for referring to a humble-bee as a 'dumble-dore' and a hyacinth as a 'greggle'. Both these dialect terms are to be found in Barnes's *Glossary*.

8 – Photographs of Mill Lane as it was may be found in Fowles, John and Draper, Jo, *Thomas Hardy's England*, Jonathan Cape, 1984, pp.141-2.

9 –2A photograph of 'The Greek Slave' will be found in Priestley, J.B., *Victoria's Heyday*, Penguin, 1974, p.78.

10 – Jones 1 pp.473-476

11 – Baxter pp. 120-121

12 – Jones 1 pp.233-4. Vaughan Williams's setting of 'Linden Lea' is said to be his most popular piece of music. The words of the song are almost certainly the most widely-known piece by Barnes even if listeners do not always know that he wrote them.

13 – Baxter 1 p.163

14 – See Hardy, Florence Emily, *The Life of Thomas Hardy*, MacMillan, 1962, p.28

15 – See Chapter XX of *The Mayor of Casterbridge*.

16 – The publication date for *Hwomely Rhymes* was the next year, i.e. 1859.

17 – Jones 1 p.171

18 – Ibid. 1 pp.252-256

19 – Ibid. 1 pp.343-344

20 – Ibid 1 pp.333-334.

21 – Baxter p.167

22 – See Pickard Cambridge, Octavius, 'In Memoriam, Rev William Barnes, B.D.' in PDNC, Vol VIII, 1887, p.xxiii.

23 – Dated 1862.

24 – Jacobs, Willis D. *William Barnes Linguist*, University of New Mexico Press, 1952, p.24.

25 – See Gardner, W.H. *Gerard Manley Hopkins*, Penguin, 1974, p.90.

CHAPTER 8

1 – See undated newspaper cuttings in a scrapbook 3, p.56, DCM.
2 – Ibid. p.13
3 – For an account of the parson-scholars of the nineteenth century see
    Colloms, Brenda, *Victorian Country Parsons*, Constable, 1977.
4 – Dugdale, p.174.
5 'Wyd was his parisshe, and houses for asonder,
    But he ne lafte nat for reyn ne thonder,
    In siknesse nor in mischief to visite
    The ferreste in his parisshe, much and lite . . .'
    Chaucer, *Prologue to the Canterbury tales*, lines 491-4
6 – Dugdale, p.198
7 – Hearl p.311
8 – Ibid.
9 – Jones 1 378-9
10 – Scrapbook 3 p.79, DCM
11 – Scrapbook 4 p.4 DCM, item dated 8th November, 1866
12 – Strictly speaking, of course, no poem is the 'same' as any other but
    there is some identity between the translation and that which is
    translated.
13 – Jones 1 532
14 – Ibid. 11 736
15 – Dugdale p.187
16 – Letter in DCM dated 18th August, 1863
17 – See Grigson, G., *William Allingham's Diary*, Centaur Press, 1967,
    p.109
18 – Ibid. p.126
19 – Ibid. pp.126-7
20 – Ibid. pp.156-7
21 – Barnes, William, *An Outline of Rede-Craft (Logic) with English
    Wording*, Kegan Paul & Co., 1880.
22 – Jacobs, op.cit. pp.64-5 and Chapter IV passim.
23 – Ibid. Chapter IV
24 – Dugdale p.206
25 – Baxter p.299
26 – Ibid. p.203
27 – See Quiller-Couch, Sir Arthur, *The Poet as Citizen*, CUP, 1934,
    pp.174-196.
28 – Dugdale p.217
29 – Ibid. p.229
30 – Jones 11 pp.928-929
31 – Dugdale p.230
32 – DCC 14/10/1886
33 – See *The Collected Poems of Thomas Hardy*, Macmillan, 1965, p.444.

Books and Pamphlets by William Barnes

POETRY

1820   *Poetical Pieces*, printed by G. Clark, Dorchester

1822   *Orra: A Lapland Tale*, printed by J. Criswick, Dorchester

1844   *Sabbath Lays: Six Sacred Songs*, Music by F.W. Smith, Chappel, London

1844   *Poems of Rural Life in the Dorset Dialect*, with a Dissertation and Glossary, John Russell Smith, London. 2nd edn. 1847, 3rd edn. 1862, 4th edn. 1866. (The 3rd and 4th edn were published with the Dissertation and Glossary).

1846   *Poems Partly of Rural Life (In National English)*, John Russell Smith, London

1859   *Hwomely Rhymes, A Second Collection of Poems in the Dorset Dialect*, John Russell Smith, London. 2nd edn. 1863.

1862   *Poems of Rural Life in the Dorset Dialect*, Third Collection, John Russell Smith, London, 2nd edn. 1869.

1864   *Poems in the Dorset Dialect*, Crosby & Nichols, Boston, Mass.

1868   *Poems of Rural Life in Common English*, MacMillan & Co., London.

1869   *Poems of Rural Life, In Common English*, Roberts Bros., Boston, Mass.

1870   *A Selection from Unpublished Poems*, the School, Winterborne Monkton, Dorchester.

1879   *Poems of Rural Life in the Dorset Dialect*, Kegan Paul & Co, London, repr. 1883, 1886, 1888, 1893, 1898, 1902, 1905.

1881   *Ruth, A Short Drama from the Bible*, H. Ling, Dorchester.

TEXTBOOKS AND MONOGRAPHS

1829   *Etymological Dictionary*, J. Rutter, Shaftesbury and Whittaker, London.

1833   *A Catechism of Government*, Charles Bastables, Shaftesbury

1833   *The Menomonic Manual* (no known copy survives)

1833   *A Few Words on the Advantages of a more common Adoption of the Mathematics as a Branch of Education of Subject of Study*, Whittaker & Co., London.

1835   *A Mathematical Investigation of the principle of Hanging Doors, Gates, Swing Bridges*, Simons and Sydenham, Dorchester.

1839   *A Corrective Concordance or Imposition Book*, G. Clark, Dorchester.

1840   *An Investigation of the Laws of Case in Language*, Longman & Co, Dorchester, and Whittaker & Co., London.

1840   *An Arithmetical And Commercial Dictionary*, Longman & Co., Dorchester, Whittaker & Co., Hamilton & Adams, London.

1842   *The Elements of English Grammar*, Longman & Co, Dorchester, Whittaker & Co., Hamilton & Adams, London.

1842   *The Elements of Linear Perspective*, Longman Brown & Co, Hamilton & Adams, London.

1844   *Exercises in Practical Science*, G. Clark, Dorchester.

1847   *Outlines of Geography and Ethnography for Youth*, Barclay, Dorchester.

1847   *Humilis Domus* (reprinted from the *Poole and Dorset Herald*)

1849   *Se Gefylsta (The Helper), An Anglo-Saxon Delectus*, John Russell Smith, London, 2nd edn. 1866.

1854   *A Philological Grammar*, John Russell Smith, London.

1858   *Notes on Ancient Britain and the Britons*, John Russell Smith, London.

1859   *Views of Labour and Gold*, John Russell Smith, London.

1859   *The Song of Soloman in the Dorset Dialect*, George Barclay, London.

1862   *TIW, or a view of The Roots and Stems of the English as a Teutonic Tongue*, John Russell Smith, London.

1863   *A Grammar and Glossary of the Dorset Dialect*, published for the Philological Society by A. Asher & Co., Berlin.

1867   *Additions from Various Sources and Notes to a Glossary, with some Pieces of Verse, of the Old Dialect of the English Colony in the Baronies of Forth and Bargy*, by Jacob Poole, now edited by William Barnes, B.D., John Russell Smith, London.

1869   *Early England and the Saxon English*, John Russell Smith, London.

1878   *An Outline of Speech-Craft*, C. Kegan Paul, London.

1880   *An Outline of Rede-Craft*, C. Kegan Paul, London.

1886   *A Glossary of the Dorset Dialect*, Maud E. Case, Dorchester and Trubner & Co., London.

Index

(Index5)